Managing
Corporate
Ethics

MANAGING
CORPORATE
ETHICS

*Learning from America's Ethical
Companies How to Supercharge
Business Performance*

FRANCIS J. AGUILAR

New York   Oxford
OXFORD UNIVERSITY PRESS
1994

Oxford University Press

Oxford   New York   Toronto
Delhi   Bombay   Calcutta   Madras   Karachi
Kuala Lumpur   Singapore   Hong Kong   Tokyo
Nairobi   Dar es Salaam   Cape Town
Melbourne   Auckland   Madrid

and associated companies in
Berlin   Ibadan

Library of Congress Cataloging-in-Publication Data
Aguilar, Francis J. (Francis Joseph)
Managing corporate ethics : learning from America's ethical companies
how to supercharge business performance/
Francis J. Aguilar.
p.   cm.   Includes index.
ISBN 0-19-508534-5
1. Business ethics—United States.
2. Business ethics—United States—Case studies.
I. Title.   HF5387.A4   1994   174'.4—dc20   93-5803

2 4 6 8 9 7 5 3 1
Printed in the United States of America
on acid-free paper

This book is dedicated to
the many talented men and women
who conduct business day in and day out
with a concern for doing what is right.

Preface

Business ethics holds a curious place in the minds and hearts of many managers. On the one hand, it stands on a pedestal, something to admire and to exhort. On the other hand, it has a negative aura, something associated with contentious problems, another brickbat for business practitioners to dodge. Along with the confusion caused by these contradictions, these managers also find themselves unsure of what is realistically achievable or how to proceed in practice. As a result, in the ongoing workings of many business organizations, the subject of business ethics is often downplayed—or even avoided.

This book is about *managing* business ethics. It does not set out to convince readers of the inherent virtues of moral rectitude. Nor does it take sides on specific ethically controversial issues. Instead, it aims to provide managers with some guidance on how to motivate ethical conduct throughout an organization and with some compelling practical reasons for doing so. The book argues that in combination with a sound business strategy, corporate ethical practices create an organizational climate capable of motivating the innovative and risk-taking initiatives that are essential to achieving and sustaining corporate excellence. In this sense, ethical standards, set by top management and fostered throughout an organization, can act to supercharge the engine of corporate performance in an already well-managed firm.

Any reader looking for a precise recipe on how to manage corporate ethics will be disappointed. Indeed, no book can prescribe what managers should do and how they should go about fostering corporate ethical behavior. The subject is too complex and the situations in individual companies are too distinctive for such an approach. What this book does is to describe what managers in ethical firms do, why they do it, and the circumstances in which they do it. Readers have to transpose these "lessons" to fit their own circumstances.

To draw realistic lessons from the experiences of companies that have committed themselves to conducting business in an ethical manner, the author interviewed people at different organizational levels and with different functional responsibilities. This was done to learn how different parts of an organization viewed business ethics and how the policies and practices espoused by senior-level managers played out at lower levels. The importance of going beyond senior managers and company spokespersons for this information is revealed in the following observation by the CEO of a large corporation. "I know what I would like to see in the way of ethical behavior in [my company]. I know what I *think* is happening. But I doubt that I really know how business ethics is viewed and practiced down in the ranks where day-to-day operations are carried out."

The findings of this study reveal much about what actually works and what does not when it comes to managing corporate ethics. They also show corporate ethics to be an exacting managerial challenge, calling for careful attention and skillful execution. Finally, they bring to light how corporate ethics, by providing employees and other stakeholders the opportunity to function in an atmosphere of mutual trust and respect, can provide business leaders with conditions favorable for promoting innovation and risk-taking so vital to corporate excellence over time.

Boston   F.J.A.
May 1993

Acknowledgments

My greatest debt of gratitude is owed to the many workers and managers who shared their thoughts and experiences regarding business ethics. They were gracious with their time and almost without exception personally interested in the subject.

I am also indebted to many people who have contributed to the making of this book:

- Professor Emeritus Kenneth R. Andrews, Professor Joseph L. Badaracco, Associate Professor J. Gregory Dees, and an unidentified reviewer for their helpful comments and words of encouragement;

- Betsy Barker, Aimée B. Hamel, and Karen E. Anderson for their outstanding word processing abilities and good cheer in reworking the manuscript countless times;

- Herbert J. Addison, Vice President–Executive Editor for Oxford University Press, for his friendly support and perceptive guidance;

- And my wife Gillian, for her common-sense reactions to the work in progress and for urging me on over the years.

F.J.A

Contents

Managing
Corporate
Ethics

1

The Supercharger of Organizational Performance

Why would corporate managers *want* to call attention to business ethics in their firms? If no one is complaining about unethical behavior, why make it an issue? After all, the pursuit of business ethics can cost money, lose sales to less scrupulous competitors, drain management time and energy, cause discontent where none existed, and give rise to unrealistic expectations as to how a corporation should or should not function. For some business leaders, the old saw, "If it ain't broke, don't fix it!" would seem particularly compelling when it comes to corporate ethics.

The problem with this thinking is that it ignores the risks and opportunity costs of not acting to ensure ethical behavior. The many publicized allegations of wrongdoing and the scandals involving business people and leading corporations are powerful reminders of the risks. Companies have been fined and their operations restricted by court orders; executives have been jailed. The legal and regulatory penalties, loss of good will in the trade, personal embarrassment, and other negative consequences that can result from misconduct provide a strong incentive for senior managements to pay at least some attention to business ethics.

There is a bright side to ethics as well. As one of the nation's leading business practitioners, James Burke, recent chairman and

3

chief executive officer of Johnson & Johnson, argued when he received the 1987 Business Statesman Award from the Harvard Business School Club of Greater New York:

> I believe there is a deep and intensely human need for trust, honesty, integrity, ethical behavior in the people we form important relationships with. Further, I believe this moral imperative *should* drive businesses to strive to satisfy that need in all of their constituencies, customers, employees, all those dependent upon them.
>
> And finally, I believe that those businesses who are the most consistently ethical in their behavior, will, on average, be more successful!

To substantiate his argument that ethical businesses are on average more successful, Burke reported on a study that showed an investment of $1,000 in each of 30 companies with higher-than-average ethical values after 30 years to have been worth 4.7 times a similar investment in a composite of the Dow-Jones ($701,150 versus $148,110). While these numbers might be open to question, the reasoning—that a commitment to ethical conduct leads to productive business relationships and brings out the best in people—rings true. Customers, suppliers, employees, and the community at large know when they are treated in a positive and constructive manner and are likely to respond in kind.

These consequences—both negative and positive—are real and important. As the following two accounts show, personal lives can be corrupted and business organizations dispirited by the willful disregard of ethical values, or, conversely, uplifted and energized by the skillful managing of corporate ethics. The stakes are high. The end results for individuals and companies can be ruinous—as the well-publicized downfalls of Michael Milken and John Gutfreund and their firms, Drexel Burnham Lambert and Salomon Brothers, so vividly illustrated—or they can be a powerful release of entrepreneurial vitality and innovative risk-taking—as the experiences of companies described in this book reveal.

A Tale of Two Companies

In June 1988, Neil L. Hoyvald and John F. Lavery, the president and vice president of Beech-Nut, were each sentenced to a prison term of a year and a day and assessed fines totaling $100,000 for their part in what was later billed as "the most serious admission of criminal wrongdoing by a major corporation," and "a classic case of big corporate greed and irresponsibility." They "had sold millions of bottles of 'apple juice' that they knew to contain little or no apple juice at all—only sugar, water, flavoring and coloring. The consumers of this bogus product were babies."[1]

Under pressure to reduce losses, Beech-Nut in 1977 abandoned its longtime supplier of apple juice concentrate for a less expensive source. In 1981, a company food scientist who had monitored the supply submitted a memorandum to management indicating a suspicion that the apple juice concentrate used to make the company's "100% fruit juice" was a blend of synthetic ingredients. At the time, no test could prove adulteration. But as a new chief executive, Hoyvald felt pressure to show an improvement in financial results to the company's new parent, Nestlé. Abandoning the low-cost supply on the basis of circumstantial evidence was out of the question. Management could take some comfort in the fact that safety was not at issue.

In 1982, such mental refuge was stripped away as the processed apple industry's trade association began to investigate charges of widespread adulteration. To avert any incrimination, Beech-Nut discontinued the use of the synthetic concentrate. Rather than incur the losses that would result from recalling and destroying the product as was urged by the firm's head of quality assurance and later by officials of the Food and Drug Administration, Hoyvald decided to sell off the company's $3.5 million inventory. In their quest to avert a major financial setback

> . . . Lavery and others [had become persuaded]—incorrectly, as it turned out—that a seizure action was imminent. After consulting with Hoyvald, executives decided to move the entire inventory of tainted juice out of the state's jurisdiction. And so, on the night of August 12, nine tractor trailers . . . were loaded with 26,000 cases of juice and taken in a ghostly caravan [from New York State] to a warehouse in Secaucus, N.J. One of America's most venerable food companies was fleeing the law like a bootlegger.[2]

Beech-Nut subsequently unloaded thousands of cases of the fake juice to Caribbean markets, while its lawyers were holding federal and state agencies at bay.

In 1987, Beech-Nut pleaded guilty to 215 counts of violating federal food and drug laws and agreed to pay a $2 million fine, by far the largest ever imposed in the 50-year history of the Food, Drug, and Cosmetic Act. Despite this admission, both senior executives pleaded not guilty and were subsequently tried.

No one would have predicted this turn of events for either of these men. Hoyvald had had an exemplary career and was respected in the industry for his previous success in turning around a faltering large food company by emphasizing quality. "Lavery was known as a figure of propriety and rectitude. 'He was as straight and narrow as anything you could come up with,' says [a colleague]. Lavery was a fixture in the Methodist church, on the school board and in community organizations."[3]

How could such upstanding people become involved in such serious illegal actions? One account of the affair gave the following answer to this question.

> The Beech-Nut employees involved were not hardened miscreants perpetrating a brazen swindle. They were honest and well-respected. Their lapse into illicit conduct required a strong catalyst: Beech-Nut was under great financial pressure, and using cheap, phony concentrate saved millions of dollars. But it also required a pernicious climate of rationalization, self-delusion, and denial. Beech-Nut executives apparently convinced themselves that what they were doing was just a little innocuous cheating.[4]

The article went on to describe the likely thinking that served to excuse the behavior.

> Evidence suggests that Beech-Nut employees used two main arguments to justify their conduct and ease their consciences. First, they believed that many other companies were selling fake juice. What, then, was so bad about Beech-Nut doing the same thing to remain competitive? Second, they were convinced that their apple juice, even if it was adulterated, was perfectly safe.[5]

The lengths to which Hoyvald and Lavery went to distort reality and to rationalize their behavior to themselves should be noted. Their decision to stand trial, despite the overwhelming case against them, was explained as follows: "because both men, by most reports, are still convinced that they committed nothing graver than a mistake in judgment. Hoyvald and Lavery seem to think of themselves as corporate patriots."[6]

This case history shows how failure to adhere to ethical standards can be a slippery slope, imperceptively and relentlessly corrupting people's values and morals. As pressures for improved financial performance mount, senior managers are motivated to lean more and more heavily on their subordinates for favorable results and to be less questioning about how they are achieved. While poor performance does not necessarily have to result in unethical behavior, it does jeopardize a firm's ability to remain on moral high ground.

The cost of unethical behavior can go well beyond legal penalties, bad press, and injured customer relations, serious as they might be. Often, the most serious consequence is the ravaging of the organizational spirit. In some instances, employees see themselves as direct victims, as when plant workers are inadequately protected in dangerous working conditions or when managers are made scapegoats for the results of poor leadership by senior executives. In other instances, they feel forced to engage in reprehensible actions, as when employees assigned to an overrun government contract are told to charge another account for which funds are still available. Resentment invariably spills over from the people directly involved to others in the organization. Some onlookers are offended by the callousness of those who appear to put self-interest above all. Some are fearful that they too might be used or abused when it serves some supervisor's interests. As these apprehensions spread, employee pride and enthusiasm give way to mistrust and discontentment, and eventually to widespread organizational malaise, and even open hostility, as revealed in the following excerpt from a letter written in 1987 by a General Motors hourly worker.

> Knowing that I never had a chance to be anything within the company, the next obvious move was for me to become active in the local union, and I did. I now had a cause . . . to screw the sons of bitches in management that had been too good to recognize me as another human being . . . I picked on bad management people and good management people. It made no difference.[7]

It would not take many people with that attitude to undermine a company's ability to function effectively.

Just as unethical behavior has the potential to ruin a firm, ethical behavior has the potential to contribute importantly to the achievement of corporate excellence. The following account shows how senior management, with the benefit of an organizational atmosphere of trust and mutual respect engendered by corporate ethical behavior, can motivate operating unit managers to be more innovative and enterprising in running their businesses.

Dover Corporation

Dover Corporation is a leading manufacturer of industrial products. The annual report listed over 40 different product families, including such items as elevators, oil pumps, valves, automated assembly equipment for printed circuit boards, toggle clamps, flow meters, automotive wreckers, parking meters, hydraulic automotive lifts, bearings, specialty seals, and commercial cooking equipment. The company's economic performance was excellent by any standard. Sales had increased from $362 million in 1976 to over $2.2 billion in 1992, earnings from $31 million to $130 million, and cash flow from $37 million to $207 million. Return on average equity was 15.9 percent.

This success was based on a powerful corporate strategy assembling a portfolio of businesses with attractive profit opportunities and motivating the managers of these operating units to work hard and do well. The ways in which Dover's high standards of ethical behavior contributed to its enviable business performance were recognized by both senior corporate and operating unit managers.

Corporate Management's Views
Dover's abilities in motivating its operating managers to achieve superior levels of performance were critical to its strategy. Gary Roubos, president and chief executive officer, described the company's basic approach:

> We believe very strongly in divisional autonomy. We make absolutely no attempt to try to run the businesses from headquarters. We see the task of top management as making sure that we always have the right person acting as company president and of spreading the knowledge of good ideas developed in one area of Dover to other areas. Our company presidents are well paid, but not lavishly. They have strong long-term incentive programs based upon the results of their own companies, and they receive 100 percent of the psychic income that comes from running a successful business. They don't get second-guessed, they don't get harassed by a lot of staff, and they don't find their bosses running in to steal their glory when things are going well.

While senior line executives were mindful not to interfere in the decisions of the operating unit managers, they did not in the least abdicate their leadership responsibilities. Rather, they saw their role as one of inspiring new initiatives, of alerting to possible dangers, and most important of selecting and supporting unit presidents. Lewis Burns, president and chief executive officer of Dover Industries, Inc. (a wholly owned subsidiary of Dover Corporation), gave some perspective to this positive approach to management in describing how he handled the eight companies reporting to him:

One of my most important responsibilities is to help people to see the possibilities open to them. People often are not imaginative and aggressive enough. Buy a competitor? Some presidents thought that was out of bounds. We asked, "Why not?" Many big companies suppress initiative and imagination by imposing excessive controls and reporting requirements on their operating units. There is little energy left for aggressive operations management when you finish fighting the bureaucracy. Dover doesn't operate that way. I see my job as being a cheerleader and encouraging people to think big.

Of course, when you find a race horse in charge of one of your companies, you don't get in the way. You just let him or her make money for the stockholders and employees.

As these comments reveal, the working assumption underlying Dover's managerial philosophy is that capable people will perform well if given a sound business and encouraged to exercise their own initiative. This approach has important ethical implications that involve trust and character. Paul Nickel, vice president of finance for Dover Industries, explained this connection:

Dover's style of decentralized operations requires an enormous amount of trust and confidence in the managers of the companies on our part. For the system of delegation to work, the corporation needs to have people with integrity, openness, a non-political nature, and self-confidence. The company does not want to have a bureaucracy to act as a watchdog over operations. That just costs money and never really works.

In making an acquisition, an enormous amount of time is spent in assessing the president. Burns, in particular, will want to find out how this person thinks and behaves. He wants to know if he or she will fit into our way of doing things, and to this end, will try hard to get to know the person's character.

The Dover style also requires that these managers have trust and confidence in senior management. To merit such trust, we have to be open with our people and we have to care about them. This has to be genuine. You can't fool people on this score for long.

This comment makes clear the importance Dover's senior management places on creating an atmosphere of trust and mutual respect as a basis for drawing out the creative energies of the organization. Great care is given to selecting people who are competent and smart. Another essential condition is that they be people of integrity. The openness that is so essential to corporate adaptiveness is carefully cultivated by senior managers in the way they deal with their subordinates and with each other.

Operating Management's Views

The importance of openness and of competence in building an atmosphere of trust is also evident in the views and experiences of
the operating unit managers. Gene Shanahan, who had left a major
industrial firm a year earlier to join Dover as president of Dieterich
Standard—a leading manufacturer of flow measurement instruments located in Boulder, Colorado, with annual sales of about $16
million and just under 100 employees—compared the two companies and noted some advantages to the more trusting environment:

> My first days of employment with Dover coincided with a bien-
> nial worldwide President's meeting. I was absolutely astounded dur-
> ing some presentations when presidents of various Dover companies
> would openly admit to problems in their businesses and even to mis-
> takes that had been made. In my prior experience, no one would
> dare to be openly critical of anyone's performance . . . especially
> one's own.
>
> In time, I came to realize that this willingness to admit openly
> to problems benefitted everyone concerned. For a company presi-
> dent, such an admission at least would gain the sympathy of those
> who understand the problem but have no solution to offer. With
> luck, someone might be able to offer helpful advice. Another benefit
> of this openness at the operating company level is in informing se-
> nior managers. They need to have a clear idea of operations—prob-
> lems as well as opportunities—in order to be comfortable with the
> way we are running the businesses and to offer guidance when pos-
> sible.

Shanahan remarked on how senior management encouraged an
open atmosphere between corporate and operating unit levels:

> Gary [Roubos] and Lew [Burns] are very accessible. There are
> very few staff people at either level, which eliminates politics and
> provides unfiltered communications. This direct contact leaves no
> room for hiding problems.
>
> Lew visits Dieterich two or three times a year. During the visits,
> he takes time to roam the facility talking with employees. There is
> no question that he cares and is interested in our business. Still, the
> responsibility for making the business work stops at my level. A
> good example of this point occurs each year in connection with our
> annual plan, which is based on what the Dieterich management be-
> lieves is possible. Lew does not approve or reject these plans. More-
> over, he does not criticize if we fall short of our goals. The manage-
> ment incentive compensation plan and professional pride motivate
> us not to fall short.

These comments by Shanahan on the importance of trust were echoed by Louise O'Sullivan, president of Groen, an old-line manufacturer of food processing and food service equipment that had been acquired by Dover in 1967.

> I know large food companies where senior people would spend two days each month reviewing operations to make sure things were right. That adds up to 24 days a year devoted to search and evasion. At Dover we skip all this because we trust each other to do the right thing.
>
> I certainly want to do the right things in my job. For one thing, I have a strong sense of personal integrity and would like to sleep at night. For another, the trust the senior people have in me also supports this sense of doing the right thing. People like Gary Roubos, Tom Sutton [Dover chairman], and Lew Burns are typical of heroes within our corporate culture. I would feel enormous shame if I could not live up to their expectations for making Groen successful in a proper way.

In this reference to "enormous shame," O'Sullivan touches on one of the most powerful motivating forces. By being entrusted with the performance and well-being of Groen and of its people, she is encouraged to internalize the corporation's high standards. Her desire for approval drives her to do a superior job in an ethical manner. This favorable motivational atmosphere rests squarely on three elements of Dover's corporate strategy: (1) putting top quality people in to head (2) healthy businesses with potential for growth and (3) giving these people encouragement and freedom to improve their units. O'Sullivan had been selected in 1985 to lead Groen because of her experience and talents. Under her command, Groen added several product lines to exploit new patterns of food consumption and took a leadership position in applying electronic control technology to conventional food processing and food service equipment. In 1992, Groen was preparing to enter the home market with a revolutionary combination convection oven and steamer that could reduce the cooking time for a large turkey from four hours to one, and produce more juicy and tender meat. This move would result in a break with Dover's corporate strategy to focus exclusively on industrial markets.

The following comment by O'Sullivan gives some idea of the sense of freedom she feels to do what is right.

> The company sells most of its equipment through distributors to the end users. Consultants are often involved in advising end

users as to what equipment to buy. Some of these consultants expect manufacturing firms to pay them something in order to have their equipment specified. Such payments are unquestionably unethical, and so Groen refuses to make them. This makes some of our distributors unhappy because sales are lost as a result of the company's position.

When asked why the company was willing to lose money for a practice that was not necessarily illegal, O'Sullivan replied,

> First, it is a bottomless well. If you pay off one, you'll have to pay off others, and the amount they ask will go up. Second, you risk losing the commitment of the consultants who do not take money. Finally, it would compromise the integrity of our company. If we start to do unethical actions in one part of our business, it sends out a strong signal that people can play games in other parts of our business. This would destroy the fabric of this company. We depend so much on being able to trust each other.

Preservation of the corporation's ethical fabric was a priority concern for Dover's senior managers. To give just one example, a decision as to whether or not to acquire a major manufacturer of parking meters with prospects for excellent profitability turned on the effect this business operation could have on Dover's ethical climate. The source of their anxiety was that payoffs might be a prevalent industry practice in competing for major municipality contracts. They did not want to expose Dover unnecessarily to corrupting influences. Moreover, they feared that a voluntary association with a morally questionable business could send a wrong message to the corporation's many operating units, undermining the high ethical standards that had been so diligently cultivated over the years. Only when Dover's CEO was convinced that such illicit practices were not common would he assent to the acquisition.

Ethics Supercharger

The stories reveal important interrelationships between business performance and corporate ethics. In Beech-Nut, we saw the corrupting influence that poor performance can engender. As a firm loses its ability to achieve its economic goals through proper and ethical business conduct, pressures begin to mount for acceptance of marginal and even unethical actions. There may be efforts to justify ethical compromises with such reasoning as "Other companies do it," and "It doesn't really hurt anyone." But, as corners get cut and people or relationships treated shabbily, the firm's reputation for integrity and fair dealing is likely to suffer.

In contrast, as we see in connection with Dover, senior management's ability to sustain high standards of corporate ethical behavior depends in no small measure on its ability to provide strong business leadership. The notion that only profitable firms can be ethical, while not quite true, reflects the important enabling function that successful business performance plays in any effort to promote corporate ethical behavior. The strong profit performance that strong business leadership is able to achieve gives management room to accept costs that might be associated with doing things morally right.

The reciprocal relationships—the impacts of ethical behavior on corporate performance—are of particular interest at this point in that they address this chapter's opening question as to why business managers should really bother themselves about corporate ethics. The potential costs of misbehaving—such as organizational resentment, loss of business, and costly litigation—are plain to see. So, too, is the generally acknowledged notion that corporate ethical behavior can strengthen a firm's productive relationships with customers, suppliers, and employees. However, this last observation, while true, generally fails to do justice to what is arguably the most important benefit that a strong commitment to high ethical standards can provide in today's tumultuous business environment— namely, to increase feelings of trust and mutual respect that are key to liberating latent innovative and entrepreneurial energies in an organization.

Consider what it takes for a company to be innovative and self-renewing over time. Clearly, it must have smart people who understand the business and are capable of foreseeing potential opportunities and threats. The presence of people with such qualities, however, is in itself not enough. They must also be willing to act and even to champion their ideas for the company to profit. But as any experienced general manager knows, major innovations and strategic decisions normally involve considerable uncertainty and business risk. They require making decisions with a limited understanding of the forces at work, challenging established views, and facing an uncertain chain of events and outcomes. They can mean upsetting established relationships with suppliers and customers, unsettling established approaches to manufacturing and marketing products, and realigning the power and influence of individual managers.

Since intended benefits of major organizational and strategic changes are generally far more uncertain than the associated costs, a case can always be made for maintaining the status quo or for making small adjustments at most. Advocating bold strategic moves and highly innovative proposals typically carries personal risks since the creative analysis can rarely be proven—depending as it does on conjectural insights and difficult judgments—and since radical changes are likely to meet with opposition. Consequently, many good ideas never see the light of day because of fears of how others might deprecate the analysis or even use the occasion to discredit the proponents. And even where bold initiatives are approved and put into play, the champion still runs the risk that the effort might fail because of inadequate organizational support, radical competitive reactions, or some other unpredictable development.

While certain organizational processes—such as the use of teams, appropriate measures of performance, and rewards for success—can encourage innovative thinking, people's willingness to stick out their necks is influenced by how they expect to be treated should difficulties arise or their proposed course of action fail to meet expectations. They must believe that their superiors respect them and will treat them in a positive and constructive manner. Consequently, to the extent that management's commitment to business ethics engenders respect and trust, it also gives rise to conditions conducive to risk-taking and innovation. Feeling valued and secure, people are more willing to put forward unconventional ideas and to engage in constructive give-and-take.

Having smart and competent people and encouraging business initiatives by reducing personal risk are essential conditions for a creative organization. But, for the new business ideas to succeed in practice, one further condition can be of vital importance in all but the smallest firms. This third condition, as evident in the Dover Corporation, is an organization disposed to cooperation and support rather than to internal suspicion, petty politicking, and strife. The advantage for corporate innovation and renewal lies not only in having the different operating units and functional departments that can contribute to an initiative provide constructive advice and encouragement during the early stages while new ideas are still imperfect and vulnerable, but also later in having them provide the active support that can be critical to a successful outcome.

Of those-mentioned three factors that energize corporate innovation and renewal—smart people, reduced personal risk, and organizational supportiveness—reduced personal risk and organizational supportiveness depend directly on an atmosphere of trust and respect. Building and maintaining organizational trust, in turn, depend on people treating each other with consideration and concern. Such behavior lies at the core of corporate ethics. And so, in effect, an ethical corporate climate can *supercharge* a well-managed and well-positioned business by helping to release creative ideas and by fostering collaborative follow-through.[8]

This supercharging effect of corporate ethics, however, does not occur spontaneously. As evident in firms that have succeeded in raising their capabilities to innovate and take risks, deliberate management effort is required to employ this powerful leverage. Chapter 7 enlarges on this consideration. The body of this book examines how business managers can bring an ethics supercharger into being by elevating an organization's commitment to ethical practices.

Understanding the Business Ethics Challenge

A comparison of firms that have been successful in motivating ethical conduct with those that have not reveals a marked difference in thinking about business ethics. A common, if not traditional, view of business ethics is that it centers on individual actions, that it is problem-oriented, and that the problems tend to be dramatic and occur occasionally, at times of unusual pressure or temptation. Most ethical violations reported in the press conform to this pattern. Moreover, in this concept, dealing with ethical issues chiefly involves the application of the appropriate moral principles and, because of the exceptional nature of these problems, is the responsibility of senior management.

In contrast, the approach and experience of ethical firms suggest a very different view of business ethics. For these firms, organizational context is a relevant consideration along with the actions of individuals; avoiding problems is as much a challenge as dealing with problems already on hand; and business ethics is seen to pertain to everyday actions, not just to major ethical dilemmas or to notorious breaches of acceptable conduct. While senior managers play a major role in promoting and implementing business ethics, people throughout these firms are also significantly involved in shaping ethical thinking. And while moral principles provide standards, those persons providing ethical leadership also rely on the wisdom of practical experience in making judgments.

The difference in the two concepts of business ethics can have major consequences with respect to what managers are motivated to do and to how organizations are likely to react. The traditional view defines a far more restricted scope for concern: managers by and large consider the organization to pass muster on business ethics as long as it is not experiencing any dramatic ethical problems. The fact that employees might resent the way they are treated or are cynical about management's intentions would not likely surface as an ethical issue. The fact that the company pulled a fast one with no one the wiser is more likely to be joked about than regretted. At the extreme, business ethics is treated something like a best Sunday outfit or formal dress, to be used only on special occasions.

The alternative concept of business ethics, evident in the ethical firms studied, is far more comprehensive in nature. It regards ethics as having pervasive relevance in that every decision and every action can have ethical consequences. These consequences can be direct, where someone's well-being is affected by the decision or action. They can also be indirect, where the impact is on the firm's moral climate. For example, a production manager's decision to rework a shipment because of marginal quality affects directly how a customer is treated. It can also make the workers involved and the whole department more conscious of doing what is right.

Clearly, the ethical challenge is far greater for managers holding an expanded view of business ethics than for those with the traditional view. Under the broader concept, minor and common instances of disrespectful treatment cause concern, as do problems waiting to happen and the conditions that might help to avoid or at least reduce such problems. As a result of this thinking, managers are motivated to be sensitive to the ethical implications of any company decision or action. They are also motivated to be sensitive to the ethical implications of any external events or developments that might be relevant to the firm in some significant way. As such, business ethics becomes another element of everyday management, along with operations and competitive strategy.

Ultimately, organizational support and commitment to corporate ethical standards will be governed by how the broadly defined ethical arena is managed. After all, most people are more directly aware of, involved with, and affected by the ethical considerations of everyday actions in the workplace than they are by the big issues. Senior managers' failure to deal effectively with commonplace ethical issues can only undermine an organization's confidence in their intentions and competence in ethical matters. Without this confidence, people cannot build the trust and enthusiasm needed to counter the many temptations and pressures of the normal business setting. In an atmosphere of distrust, business ethics is practiced with caution or indifference, if at all.

In effect, business ethics must be considered in its broad definition if it is to have real meaning for corporate behavior. Management must be concerned with and also be effective in dealing with the ethical dimensions of everyday decisions and actions as well as the so-called big issues if it is to provide moral leadership.

Learning from the Experience of Ethical Firms

A company planning to enter unfamiliar business waters—opening operations in Eastern Europe, for example, or employing a new manufacturing technology—typically would turn for advice to firms and people who have been successful in related experiences. This common-sense approach also applies to the challenge of managing business ethics. What is needed is useful information about how firms that have succeeded in promoting ethical behavior in their business operations approach and manage business ethics, and the consequences of their efforts. Fortunately, such information can be obtained.

Some people question the idea of an ethical business firm, calling the expression an oxymoron. And indeed, no business firm of an appreciable size and complexity can escape involvement with ethical misconduct of one kind or another. But such misconduct is likely to be far less serious and frequent for firms in which senior management provides effective ethical leadership than for those in which it fails to address the issue, or, worse yet, is motivated solely by self-interest.

An ethical business firm is defined for our purposes as an enterprise that has earned the respect and trust of its employees, customers, suppliers, investors, and others by striking an acceptable balance between its economic interests and the interests of all parties affected when making decisions and taking actions. The companies in this book meet this criterion. None is without its ethical shortcomings. But each has achieved a clear measure of success in promoting an organizational sensitivity to ethical issues and a commitment to ethical conduct. Individually, they can teach us how to manage corporate ethics. Collectively, they allow us to envisage a model of the ethical business firm.

The principal sources of information were Armstrong World Industries, Cray Research, Dover Industries, General Mills, Hewlett-Packard, Johnson & Johnson, Lincoln Electric, Mark Twain Bancshares, ServiceMaster, and Texas Instruments. Another ten firms—including Dow-Jones, Procter & Gamble, Goldman Sachs, Nucor Steel, and Norton—also provided information on a more limited basis. The selection of firms was guided by the desire to include variety in size, complexity, and line of business. In keeping with this criterion, the firms range in size from medium to quite large and in the diversity of their operations from a single business to over 30 businesses. They also represent a wide variety of industries, including packaged foods, health care products, industrial equipment, defense electronics, housing materials, supercomputers, banking, and industrial cleaning services.

The particular mix of ethical problems and concerns differ from company to company, reflecting size, business, people, and history. Specific actions and general approaches correspondingly differ. Nonetheless, there are patterns and similarities in the way the companies go about motivating organizational responsiveness to ethical considerations. This comparability of experiences across a broad range of contexts indicates that these companies can provide valuable lessons for those managers who take on the formidable challenge of business ethics.

Despite the many distinctive features of the various approaches to business ethics followed by these companies, all demonstrated two important capabilities in common. Simply put, one was in avoiding ethical problems wherever possible, and the other in dealing effectively with those ethical problems that arose.

Avoiding Ethical Problems
The ethical firm is one where employees are motivated as a matter of course to behave ethically in their work. Many ethical problems are avoided because people become skilled in taking into account the interests of all parties affected by each business decision or action. As a result of deliberate corporate decisions to stay clear of potentially troublesome situations, other ethical problems never arise. It is not surprising that the easiest and most effective way to deal with ethical problems is not to have them in the first place. The aphorism "An ounce of prevention is worth a pound of cure" applies as much to moral as to physical well-being.

The ethical firms included in this study were very good at encouraging ethical behavior and discouraging unethical behavior. As a result, they were able to eliminate many of the costly hassles and much of the demoralizing impact that ethical problems can inflict on corporations in the course of normal business operations.

Resolving Ethical Problems
No matter how hard it tries, management can never succeed completely in avoiding ethical problems. Human weakness, the inherently perplexing nature of some ethical situations, and the emergence of unanticipated ethical issues are some of the reasons why ethical breakdowns and confrontations arise in even the most high-minded corporate settings.

The ethical firms studied were skillful in dealing with ethical problems that could not be avoided or anticipated. Their skills in this regard embraced an ability for recognizing and acknowledging the moral difficulties that they had experienced and an ability for responding appropriately. Every effort was made to satisfy all parties concerned, if not totally, at least as a best-possible solution reflecting a diligent and fair-minded effort.

Business ethical leadership depends on senior management's success both in avoiding and resolving ethical problems. Without the moderating effect of a well-established moral corporate culture, the number and nature of troublesome ethical problems can escalate beyond management's capacity to solve them. Conversely, contentious ethical problems serve as litmus tests of management's ethical resolve. An inability or unwillingness to put them to rest calls into question management's commitment and capability, undermining an otherwise well-managed business ethics process; successful handling provides valuable confirmation and reinforcement of these critical qualities.

Managing the Business Ethics Process

A company's ability to avoid ethical problems that can be avoided, to deal with those that either cannot be or mistakenly are not avoided, and to create an organizational atmosphere of trust and mutual respect requires deliberate and skillful managing that is ongoing and pervasive. As the experiences of the firms studied reveals, the task of managing what can be called the business ethics process calls for action on four principal fronts.

Developing Ethical Sensitivity. The first of these actions is for senior managers to become informed about the nature of the business ethics challenge and sensitive to the ethical issues relevant to their firm. For starters, senior managers must be aware of the common difficulties that can impede ethical leadership. These difficulties, capable of derailing well-intentioned efforts, are not necessarily obvious to someone—even a seasoned business executive—who has had little exposure to managing corporate ethics.

Senior managers must also develop a sensitivity to the specific moral issues that affect or threaten their firms. Without this sensitivity, they can unwittingly cause or allow improper conduct to take place. Such unethical actions are no less objectionable to the injured party or in the eyes of others—and therefore no less destructive of people's trust in senior management's moral integrity—just because they fall outside of management's ethical consciousness.

Strong Competitive Strategy and Operating Management. The second prerequisite action in the business ethics process is for senior management to ensure that the business is well managed in all other respects. Among the companies observed, those with the most favorable ethical climate also enjoyed strong business leadership. Poor operating performance invites cutting close to the line of acceptable behavior—and even crossing it—to avoid the consequences of failure. Under pressure from the board of directors or from threats of takeover, even senior managers with the best of intentions can fall prey to the lures and tyranny of the bottom line. In contrast, strong and effective management makes it easier to behave ethically when the organization can achieve its financial goals through upright business practices. Strong and effective management is also critical to tap the creative and adventurous spirit of the organization once the prerequisite trust and mutual respect have been developed.

A Business Ethics Program. With a foundation of ethical sensitivity and a well-directed business in place, senior management is in a position to promote ethical behavior throughout the firm, the third element in the framework for managing corporate ethics. The basic considerations of a sound business ethics program involve the development of policies and organizational arrangements that promote organizational concern for the interests of the different parties affected by the firm's operations and provide safeguards against corrupting business pressures. This basic framework must be supported and extended by a wide variety of actions and practices. Examples of management's efforts to nurture an organization's ethical values would include giving inspirational talks, offering ethical training, setting good examples, disciplining misconduct, and being responsive to employees who are concerned or confused about ethical issues.

Ethical People. The fourth component of the business ethics process is to staff and surround an organization with ethical people. The staffing consideration calls for recruiting people with strong moral values (and rejecting candidates lacking in this respect), helping employees to connect their personal values to their work activities, and placing people skillful in providing moral leadership in positions where such leadership can have greatest effect on others in the organization. Surrounding the organization with ethical people requires that moral values be an important consideration in the selection of professional advisors (legal, financial, accounting, tax, advertising, management consultation, and the like), suppliers, associated companies (distribution, joint venture partner, etc.), and where appropriate (such as certain areas of industrial marketing), even customers.

The managerial actions described above and depicted in Exhibit 1–1 complement and reinforce each other in creating an organiza-

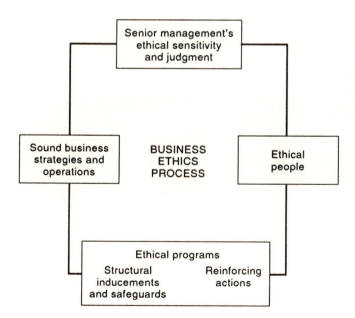

Exhibit 1–1 Actions to manage corporate ethics

tional bias that fosters ethical behavior and discourages misconduct and unfair actions. Together they constitute a comprehensive approach to managing corporate ethics.

This book examines each of the principal managerial actions. Chapter 2 describes special difficulties managers face in promoting corporate ethical conduct and how ethical sensitivity and judgment can be enhanced. Chapters 3 and 4 discuss ethical programs, starting with a look at a firm's formal structure of policies and procedures to induce ethical behavior and to discourage misconduct and then discussing the various ways in which senior managers reinforce and nurture organizational commitment to ethical practices. Chapter 5 is concerned with issues having to do with developing ethical leadership for the firm. Since the major point concerning sound strategic and operating management is to highlight the important enabling role that excellent commercial and financial results play in fostering corporate ethical behavior and not specifically to instruct on business administration, this particular dimension is touched on throughout the book instead of in a separate chapter. The special considerations associated with introducing a corporate ethics program and engaging the *supercharging* leverage that an ethical corporate climate can offer to advance innovation and risk-taking in an organization are discussed in the final two chapters.

For many executives, the managerial challenge associated with corporate ethics can be unlike anything they have ever experienced. Developing an ethical modus operandi takes more time than they anticipate or are willing to grant. Moreover, the task is never fully accomplished; setbacks are bound to occur and forces of erosion are continually at work. It is also easy to accept superficial and inflated results at face value, undermining the foundations of the whole business ethics process. In managing business ethics, results are not proportional to effort—half-measures are more likely to result in lost ground than in half-progress. Business ethics is one of those managerial endeavors where it is important to get it right the first time.

2

Starting with Informed Leadership

One of the most striking characteristics common to the ethical firms studied is senior management's deep and enduring commitment to the organizational achievement of high ethical standards. What is also evident is that such commitment, to be effective, requires more than just good intentions. These intentions must be grounded in an understanding of the problem, of the forces involved, and of the possible outcomes. Only when management's *good* intentions are also *informed* intentions is it in a position to create a corporate context that motivates and supports ethical behavior. Senior managers have to straighten out their own thinking and actions before they can straighten out the thinking and actions of their people.

Unfortunately, many business leaders who acknowledge business ethics as relevant to their firms' operations fall prey to underestimating the difficulties associated with developing true organizational commitment to this cause. This error perhaps has done more to undermine progress in the cause of business ethics than anything else. Overlooked in this framing of the problem is the question of top management's competence and credibility in these matters. In effect, these business leaders behave as though they know exactly what needs to be done, never questioning the quality of their own understanding. For them, the goal is simply to ensure that others in the organization know and commit to their views.

But this thinking is likely to be presumptuous. There is no reason for business practitioners—even able and mature executives—to have any special competence in moral reasoning.[1] Nor are they necessarily prepared to deal with the subtleties and complexities inherent in any effort to promote ethical behavior in a business organization. Further complicating the challenge, managers—even those who are competent to deal with business ethics—face a need to establish their credibility in this regard. Employees are likely to have less confidence in senior management's competence and intentions regarding business ethics than they would in its abilities to direct marketing, finance, or production and its commitment to make profits. In such circumstances, even sound management actions in ethical matters will command less organizational support than senior managers might be accustomed to in their normal administrative dealings.

This chapter examines some of the special difficulties that senior managers might face in attempting to provide ethical leadership to their corporation. The following disguised account of a medium-sized, defense industry company seeking to upgrade the management of ethical behavior gives some idea of how top-level company executives with good intentions can be unwittingly counterproductive in acting with inadequate forethought and preparation. As is often the case, the ill-fated approach appears sensible on the surface.

Off to a Bad Start

In early May 1989, John Richards, chief executive officer of Cybersyn Systems Incorporated (CSI), met with Jay Wahlrig, chairman, to discuss the company's ethical standards.[2] Richards had just received word that a CSI technical sales representative had been implicated in an investigation of an Army procurement official at the U.S. Army Communication Electronics Command at Fort Monmouth, New Jersey. While the alleged violation concerning entertainment was thought to be minor, if even true, Richards and Wahlrig were seriously concerned. Their concern was motivated by high personal standards of integrity as well as by the serious nature of the risks the company faced in connection with possible misconduct in defense procurement.

They concluded that CSI "had to tighten up its rules." According to Wahlrig, Cybersyn's existing code of conduct, which had served the company well for almost 10 years, no longer was adequate to deal with the present and emerging requirements for the defense industry. In line with the decision to upgrade the company's ethical standards, Wahlrig instructed his senior staff assistant, Janet Stahlmann, to survey industry practices. As an interim measure, Richards invoked a total prohibition against any expenditures for entertaining government officials.

Stahlmann attended a two-day forum on business ethics to begin her investigation. The program included speakers from Department of Defense procurement and criminal investigation agencies and from General Motors, IBM, Texas Instruments, and TRW as models for effective corporate implementation of industry-sanctioned practices. She next collected sample copies of corporate business ethics statements, codes of conduct, training manuals, communication guides, and related materials that were considered model specimens or were employed by companies similar to CSI in size and business mission. Working with Wahlrig, Stahlmann then spent two weeks preparing a proposal for a business standards program for CSI. The major elements of the program were concerned with a code of conduct, communications, training, and a system of internal controls.

So far, the situation at CSI appears quite promising. The two most senior managers, who have led the corporation almost 35 years, have strong moral values and run the business accordingly. A potentially serious ethics problem grabs their attention and galvanizes them into action. A competent and experienced senior staff member gathers considerable information about the practices and experiences of companies that serve as models for managing business ethics. The chairman actively provides direction to the study. In effect, CSI is following a textbook approach. And yet, a careful look at the process reveals that it has serious flaws.

One problem was senior management's failure to think through what it wants to achieve in upgrading the company's ethical standards. A query to Wahlrig and Stahlmann as to their objectives for the proposed program elicited the following comments:

WAHLRIG: We want to stay out of trouble. It is necessary in today's defense industry environment for a company to be able to show that it had taken proper precautions regarding ethical conduct should any questionable practice be uncovered.

STAHLMANN: I think more in terms of our wanting to be perceived by employees, customers, and other outsiders as the ethical company that we are.

WAHLRIG: Good point. The fact of the matter is that we really do try

to be ethical in our business dealings. This program should help us
to do a better job along these lines.

This exchange reveals three quite different objectives. The first
comment stresses an exculpatory perspective. The principal concern appears to be one of clearing the company from blame in the
event of misconduct by one or more of its employees. The second
comment focuses on projecting a favorable corporate image. Unlike
the first comment's defensive perspective, this one imparts a more
positive tone and has a broader reach in terms of audience and
scope. The third comment places emphasis on how the company
can improve organizational behavior. CSI management, motivated
to act by the allegation concerning a violation of contracting regulations, remains unclear about its objectives for the ethics program.
Without clear purpose, management is illpositioned to proceed
further.

A second failing was in the way senior management went
about developing the understanding and expertise that it would
need to bring about changes in the corporation's commitment to
higher ethical standards. The staff member selected to help the
chairman had little prior experience with the problems of managing business ethics and was given little time to develop any expertise. Her information came almost exclusively from external
sources. Not surprisingly, the resulting program was largely copied
from other companies, with little tailoring for CSI's special needs.
The possible misfit between the adopted program and CSI's normal
ways of doing things, however, was not necessarily the most serious negative consequence. Stahlmann's approach did little to discover what other ethical problems—real or perceived—might be
troubling CSI employees. As a result, the company was poorly prepared to deal with such issues in a timely and informed manner.

CSI top management also failed to create conditions favorable
for gaining widespread commitment. Stahlmann's focus on outside
sources of information not only restricted learning, it also denied
operating managers the opportunity to gain any sense of ownership
in the ethical program. The program in effect became a top-down
intervention. What made it worse was the negative tone of the
code of conduct. While the preamble addresses ethics in broad, positive terms, the body of the document is dedicated largely to what
employees must learn and what they must do and not do. In effect,
the standards—covering such considerations as product quality,
sales and marketing, negotiations, finance and billing practices—

describe the legal and ethical conduct expected of all employees and define conduct the company regards as unethical. Little or no attention is given to how the company might attempt to reduce the pressures and temptations that motivate unethical behavior, or to how senior management intends to become more knowledgeable and sensitive with respect to ethical matters. It would be easy for the engineers and other employees to perceive the ethics program as a way to protect the company with little personal benefit to them. Indeed, the detailed documentation and the legalistic procedures (such as requiring employees to sign statements acknowledging that they have read and understood the code of conduct) that CSI intended to adopt were likely to confirm such suspicions.

Notwithstanding the high moral values and good intentions of the senior managers, CSI appears poised to take a step backward rather than forward in attempting to move in the direction of higher ethical standards. Indeed, management's sense of outrage and urgency might have caused it to act too hastily. As a result, the proposed effort is more likely to evoke resentment and mistrust in the organization than interest and enthusiasm.

CSI's story is not uncommon. Shaping the ethical character of the firm is not something most corporate managements have much experience with. Mistakes are easy to make. Unfortunately, ethical mistakes cannot be reversed as easily as economic mistakes. A ten million dollar operating loss is canceled out by a ten million dollar gain; a person or firm caught in deception will not come out even by telling the truth the next time. The record of ethical failures tends to be written in indelible ink.

Impediments to Ethical Leadership

In Chapter 1, ethical leadership was said to rest on management's abilities for avoiding ethical problems wherever possible and in dealing effectively with those ethical problems that do arise. The task of motivating organizations to behave ethically, however, turns out to be a far more difficult and demanding managerial challenge than most managers anticipate. As revealed in the CSI account, management's failure to understand the special difficulties involved and to take them into account is likely to impair severely its abilities to bring about a profound and lasting improvement in a firm's ethical conduct. These difficulties include: problems in recognizing and defining the relevant ethical issues; a lack of agreement as to what constitutes an appropriate response to ethical issues in business; an inherent intractability of many ethical problems; and a general reluctance to discuss moral issues.

Hidden and Misconstrued Ethical Issues

As the following two accounts show, ethical issues can be difficult to recognize for what they are. The first—the Burlington Northern Railroad Company's decision in 1986 to develop a computer-assisted logistics cost analysis program for marketing purposes—reveals the many potential ethical considerations that can be embedded in a seemingly ethically neutral activity. The analytical model was to show customers the cost advantage of rail transport over trucking when the entire logistics cycle (including costs for in-transit, cycle, and safety inventory stocks as well as for transportation) was taken into account. Each sales representative would perform the necessary calculations on a laptop computer in the customer's office.

Few managers would think to examine this kind of ordinary business decision with a critical eye for its ethical implications. And yet, the introduction of Burlington Northern's ShipSmart™ program has a variety of possible ethical consequences. For example, since the logistics model was to be a major marketing tool, its designers might be tempted or induced to bias the analytical construct to favor rail transport. (While the model was designed to be "user friendly," it was sophisticated in its internal structure, employing elaborate algorithms to deal with the complexities of the logistics analysis.) Similarly, what is to prevent an aggressive Burlington Northern sales representative from using input data and assumptions that favor rail transport when the most appropriate numbers might lose an important account? The definitive outputs of the analytical program—$X total costs for rail versus $Y for trucks—increased the opportunities for misrepresentation when compared to the previous sales methods based on a blend of ballpark numbers and bonhomie.

The customer was not the only party at risk. What happens to the sixty-two-year-old sales representative who has been selling rail service for over thirty years on the basis of personal relationships and who has never used a computer when the company requires him to do computing on his customer's desk? What if this person is unable to master the new approach? Clearly, some employees could be hurt by the decision, raising further ethical questions.

The new decision support system, in calling attention throughout the Burlington Northern organization to customers' needs, also had favorable consequences with respect to the firm's ethical climate in at least two significant ways. First, the program helped to break down barriers between operations, sales, and engineering. Prior to its inception, the operations and engineering departments, insulated from customer pressures, had tended to be driven by their costs and by the convenience of the status quo. As far as they were concerned, the sales department was responsible for peddling the available services. The sales department, in turn, was constantly pressured to satisfy customers' demands under highly competitive conditions. The result of this compartmental separation was divisive and promoted self-interest. The increasingly constructive interactions between departments engendered by the new customer orientation strengthened personal relations and organizational morale. Second, by highlighting service deficiencies, the new program became an important factor in motivating operational changes that strengthened Burlington Northern's competitive stance. The resulting improvements in financial performance should in time bring about a healthier organization, and consequently a more favorable setting for managing corporate ethics.

The business decision to introduce a computer-assisted logistics cost analysis program as a marketing tool had important ethical implications, whether or not management was aware of them. Indeed, most corporate activities are likely to have hidden ethical dimensions, and management's failure to search them out can be costly. Painful ethical problems might be avoided, or at least reduced, if detected early. Similarly, opportunities to strengthen the ethical climate of the organization—as described for Burlington Northern—can best be exploited with foresight. But managers must be sensitive to these possibilities if they are to fulfill their ethical responsibilities.

In contrast to the above illustration regarding hidden ethical issues, the next account touches on the difficulty managers can have in defining correctly what might seem to be straightforward ethical problems. A large firm, that must remain anonymous, closed a plant and laid off its work force for business reasons (the product was selling poorly and showed little promise for improvement). Management, justifiably proud of its traditional concern for the company's people, was deeply troubled by the painful consequences of discontinued employment and took care to carry out the closure with compassion for the workers affected. They were given three to four months notice, awarded generous severance pay based on length of service, and assisted to find new employment in the community. Moreover, they were offered a priority status with respect to new hiring in the company's other plants in that community. Management looked back on this experience with pride, especially since all the workers in good standing were offered the opportunity to resume employment in the company within three years.

Viewed in the way management looked at the situation—"We have to close the plant, so let's treat the workers right in doing so"—the actions are a model of ethical concern. But viewed more broadly, it is not at all clear that the company's responsibilities and its field of action should have been delimited in the way they were. When the reason for closing the plant is considered, management must take some blame for failing to position the product line to compete effectively. Since there was no major, unexpected, external development to blame, the reason for failure clearly rested more heavily on management's shoulders than on those of the workers. In this situation, one might question whether the company did not have a greater responsibility for the workers' welfare than simply softening a blow that possibly need never have been inflicted in the first place. The plant managers and supervisory people were all transferred to other plants. Did not the company owe this consideration to its workers as well? Should the plant have been assigned another product to keep it going? Could the product have been phased out more slowly to give time for transfers and natural attrition to take effect?

As this example reveals, the ethical implications of a business problem can be difficult to determine. Experienced business people of good will might easily disagree in their answers to the questions posed.[3] Management's failure in this instance was not so much in its answers to these questions as it was in not even asking them. Its truncated view of the situation, in effect, failed to include what might have been the most important ethical issues. In defining ethical issues, managers have to try to understand how their decisions and actions are likely to appear to each of the parties affected.

Developing ethical sensitivity—an ability to recognize and define ethical issues—is among the most important requirements for effective ethical leadership.

Conflicting Guides for Action

Even in those cases where there is agreement on the ethical significance of a particular issue, disagreement on how business should act can confound the interested parties. These disagreements might reflect different opinions about the proper role of business in dealing with ethical problems or different moral outlooks.

Role of Business

In a survey predominantly of directors and officers of corporations with $500 million or more in annual sales, opinions diverged widely as to the best measure for encouraging ethical behavior. Almost 40 percent of the 1,082 respondents favored adoption of business codes, 30 percent an improved curriculum in business education, 20 percent legislation, and the remainder a variety of other answers.[4] While the complexity of the issue is probably sufficient reason to explain the lack of agreement, it is interesting to note that the answers reflect different views on the role of business in this matter. The first group appears to assign prime responsibility for ensuring ethical behavior to business itself. The other two principal groups look to outside agents for corrective actions—educational institutions to give instruction and government to define rules and impose sanctions.

This kind of disagreement reflects fundamental differences in how business practitioners view the connection between business and ethics.[5] One view holds that business success—usually defined as making profits over the long term—is management's sole responsibility. Preserving amicable relations with employees, customers, and other parties is done only to the extent that it benefits business performance. This attitude is described and advanced by an experienced business consultant in the following argument:

> . . . as long as a company does not transgress the rules of the game set by law, it has the legal right to shape its strategy without reference to anything but its profits. If it takes a long-term view of its profits, it will preserve amicable relations, so far as possible, with those with whom it deals. A wise businessman will not seek advantage to the point where he generates dangerous hostility among employees, competitors, customers, government, or the public at large. But decisions in this area are, in the final test, decisions of strategy, not of ethics.[6]

The author claimed this view of business ethics as prevailing in the business community. While it is difficult to substantiate this claim either as of the time it was made or at present, anyone who follows the press about illegal and unethical corporate actions knows that this mindset must be alive and kicking. At the extreme, even compliance with the law depends only on the net expected cost versus benefit. In such cases, when the potential rewards are high and the likelihood of being caught or the penalties are small, the law is deliberately violated.

A second view treats respect for others as a legitimate and even a desirable constraint on self-interest, but one that needs to be defined for and imposed on business by outside forces. According to this thinking, the boundaries of behavior should be determined by laws and regulations as well as by the ability of parties involved in a company's transactions to invoke sanctions—for example, customers and suppliers can stop dealing with an excessively self-serving company; employees can leave an unfair employer or can retaliate in various ways.

A third view regards respect for others to be as important as economic performance in the manager's operating consciousness. This way of thinking would have companies strive to achieve high standards of ethical behavior, reaching beyond the obligations defined by law and even beyond the norms set by convention when it is the right thing to do.

When managers disagree on the nature of a firm's moral responsibility, the already difficult task of achieving high standards of ethical behavior can become impossible. The survey results noted earlier and common experience indicate that all three mindsets are widely accepted in the business world. Conflicting views as to how business should regard moral considerations unquestionably contribute to people's confusion in thinking about business ethics and weaken organizational efforts to raise standards of behavior.

Moral Outlooks
Moral philosophy offers a variety of ways to organize ethical analysis.[7] These philosophical frameworks can differ, sometimes quite markedly, in defining the moral content of a specific situation and the appropriate course of action. Consequently, even people of a mind to foster ethical behavior can be frustrated by conflicting views on how to resolve an ethical problem. For example, one com-

pany's senior managers struggled among themselves in trying to decide what to do about employees who were found guilty of substance abuse. One group advocated termination on the grounds that these people had violated a basic, well-publicized corporate policy—as well as the law, in many cases. To do otherwise, they reasoned, would undermine the deterrent force of the policy and lead to further violations. A second group favored offering such employees an opportunity to attend a rehabilitation program at company expense and to be reinstated on successful completion. One view is not necessarily right and the other wrong in order to act ethically in this case. These opposing positions reflect different valid moral outlooks.

Further complicating the ability of managers to communicate with each other about ethical considerations are differences in their individual capacities to reason in such matters. According to theories on development of the human psyche, people are capable of developing morally, much as they do physically and intellectually.[8] While the scholars of moral philosophy might differ on their definitions of moral reasoning, they generally agree that moral development, unlike physical growth, does not progress automatically, so that people who are comparable in age and intellect might be quite different in their moral maturity. The resulting differences in moral reasoning can cause colleagues to disagree as to what is at issue and how to deal with it.

Ethical Dilemmas

Managers who are sensitive to the ethical content of business decisions and operational activities, who agree to behave ethically, and who hold compatible views on how to analyze ethical situations still must confront the inherently perplexing nature of many ethical problems. As one study of business ethics observed: "As managers talked about ethical problems in their work, it was clear that what they were describing were *dilemmas*, situations in which they were faced with a difficult choice and where no clear-cut right answers existed."[9] Such dilemmas can lead to honest differences of opinion among sincere and virtuous people and to frustration for an individual trying to do the right thing.

The following disguised case illustrates the quandary managers can face. Over a period of several years, a number of salespeople in one division of a large, multibusiness corporation had substituted a cheaper chemical for the item ordered to lower the division's costs and raise its profits. When corporate management uncovered this illegal practice, it immediately ordered its cessation and corrected flaws in the control system.

An investigation uncovered the following facts. The practice had been widespread, involving hundreds and possibly thousands of accounts. In many cases it was impossible for the company to determine whether a customer had been cheated because prices were typically negotiated informally, with orders often placed by phone and field sales records poorly kept. Projecting from those instances where substitution was detected, investigators estimated that the overcharges to customers might have exceeded $1 million. They also concluded that damage to any one customer was relatively small. The substituted product, although cheaper, was thought to have performed as well as and possibly even better than what had been ordered. The substitution was virtually impossible to detect without special laboratory testing. There was evidence that the senior divisional managers, who were no longer with the company, had condoned and even encouraged the practice. The salespeople involved had apparently not gained any direct remuneration from their misdeeds.

Senior management acknowledged that the restitution of the over-charges would be the right thing to do. But there were many problems with this approach. The division's faulty records meant that it would be necessary to involve customers in the investigation. Since many, if not most, customers had not been victims, such a course of action would tarnish the company's reputation and harm shareholders and employees should future orders and sales be unfavorably affected. The reputation of innocent salespersons could also be damaged. And in the victimized companies, purchasing agents and plant supervisors might be unfairly punished because they had not detected the product substitution.

No longer is the correct course of action so obvious. Restitution of the unearned money is morally correct. Avoiding harm to innocent individuals is also morally correct. It is not clear how the company can honor both principles. Deciding whose claims have priority and how to balance the various rights can lead to considerable soul searching on the part of managers who would like to do the right thing. Any decision is likely to leave one or more injured parties and a sense of dissatisfaction and a residue of guilt for the decision makers.

Reluctance to Discuss Moral Issues

Yet another impediment to corporate ethics is a general reluctance business practitioners have to discussing moral issues. For example, in my experience at board meetings, any mention of a possible ethical violation on the part of someone in the company, especially one involving a person known to the directors, generally evokes feelings of discomfort among those present. Words are carefully chosen, opinions offered tentatively. It is a subject usually raised with reluctance, if raised at all.

This reluctance to discuss moral considerations openly—a phenomenon Bird and Waters call *moral muteness*[10]—has many reasons and is far more pervasive in business organizations than just at the board level. They point out that many managers consider it disruptive to bring up moral issues at work, noting, "In the case of moral questions, managers find confrontations particularly difficult because they experience them as judgmental and likely to initiate cycles of mutual finger-pointing and recrimination." They also observe, "In addition, managers shun moral talk because such talk seems to result in burdening business decisions with considerations that are not only extraneous, but at times antagonistic to responsible management." In this connection, many managers are said to associate ethics with rigid rules and intrusive regulations. Finally, ambitious managers, seeking to project an image of power and business savvy, avoid discussing ethical considerations because it might make them appear idealistic and naive. Moreover, such moral talk can easily appear to others as moralistic and self-serving.

Left unattended, this behavior tends to be rationalized and suppressed. By avoiding moral talk, managers remain unclear about how to cope with difficult ethical problems and about their obligations to act in accordance with moral standards. To avoid the stress that such uncertainties might cause, they are motivated to suppress the troublesome moral dimensions in business decisions.[11] They can do this by mindlessly following common practice or company directives, or by redefining the moral issues as matters of technique or taste. This reluctance to address moral issues openly is likely to go unperceived by people in the organization. The reasons for this, according to one scholarly observer, have to do with normal human and organizational behavior:

> Whenever human beings are faced with any issue that contains significant embarrassment or threat, they act in ways that bypass, as

best they can, the embarrassment or threat. In order for the bypass to work, it must be covered up.

Because most individuals use these actions, the actions become part of the fabric of everyday life. And because so many individuals use these actions frequently, the actions become organizational norms. The actions come to be viewed as rational, sensible, and real-istic.[12]

These defensive reactions are difficult to combat because they occur imperceptibly, even unwittingly. As noted above, to admit covering up an embarrassing or threatening issue is in itself embarrassing, and so people tend to cover up to themselves the cover up. As applied to moral considerations, an organization imperceptively comes to regard business ethics as taboo.

Enhancing Ethical Sensitivity

In the face of these serious impediments to ethical leadership—the difficulties in recognizing and defining relevant ethical issues, in determining the proper role of business, in deciding on moral guidelines, in resolving dilemmas, and in dealing with reluctance to discuss moral issues—what is an otherwise preoccupied senior executive to do? The answer is not simple.

Managers can employ a wide variety of sources for information to inform themselves about business ethics. Newspapers, business publications, industry conferences, special studies, and other public sources of information are helpful in signaling trends and new developments that might introduce new issues for ethical consider-ations or alter how people think about existing issues. Customers, suppliers, community leaders, business associates, friends, and family are other valuable sources. Apart from any information of a general nature that they might provide about business ethics, these parties often are able to call attention to ethical issues of particular relevance to the firm or to give distinctive views as to what is at stake or how to act. Many of the most important sources of infor-mation about company-specific ethical issues, not surprisingly, are to be found inside the firm.

Encouraging Free and Open Discussion

Evidence from the more than 20 companies studied would lead one to conclude that managers who are most successful in uncovering relevant moral issues in their business activities are those who, by their interest and receptivity, invite this kind of information from others. One such person is John Dubinsky, chief executive officer of Mark Twain Bancshares, who described his efforts to assure his organization's ethical concern for the communities it served:

> In my view, top management has a responsibility to take positions concerning the conduct of the organization. A commercial bank like ours has a moral responsibility in its role as steward for community funds. In effect, this bank acts as a gatekeeper for what happens and what does not happen in our community by its decisions as to which activities are to be funded and which are not.
>
> To make informed judgments in these matters, I talk to the officers and to outsiders who have knowledge about the facts or expertise about the issues. These things get talked over at board meetings, with employees, and with people in the community before I take a position.

Instructing his people about the company's positions on these issues provided Dubinsky with further opportunity to expand his thinking about the bank's ethical responsibilities. He explained:

> When the issue is black and white, the bank has an answer and will give it. In the gray areas, we tell our people, "If you find a proposition that makes you uncomfortable as to its reputability, you probably have as good a definition as any as to whether it is ethical and as to whether the bank wants to do that business."
>
> I take every opportunity I can to talk to my people about this, especially those who have recently joined us. The best way to raise these issues, I find, is through specific examples. For example, if the bank were asked to lend money for the financing of a pornographic shop, would this be okay? What about an abortion clinic? As it is, the bank does have a policy against making a loan for a porno shop, but its position concerning the abortion clinic is undecided. In the discussions on abortion clinics, we get strong feelings both ways. I find that helpful. Indeed, the goal of these talks is not so much to state company policy as it is to make our officers—and that includes me—more sensitive to the ethical dimensions of our business.

Dubinsky's remarks reveal two important considerations concerning free and open discussion about ethical matters. One is the importance for senior managers to interact on an ongoing basis with as many people as possible. Misconduct and injustice—willful or unintended—can occur anywhere in a business organization. For this reason, anyone in the organization can be the best or sometimes only source of information about an important ethical issue.

The other point involves the focus of discussion. While the manner in which different senior managers gain insight about ethical issues from people in their company varies with circumstances and personal style, the degree to which the most effective communicators think in terms of specifics rather than principles is striking. In discussing corporate ethics, people like Ken Iverson, chairman and CEO of Nucor, and Gary Roubos, CEO of Dover, invariably would speak to actual issues of direct concern to their organizations. For them, the desire to do the right thing makes most sense in a specific context. By focusing on concrete business issues, relevance is readily established. By avoiding moral abstractions, the senior manager is less likely to be perceived as preaching or engaging in ideological posturing. Waters and Bird go so far as to argue that moral standards "gain clarity and authority only as they are interpreted in relation to specific relevant cases."[13]

Obviously, some business leaders are more approachable and outgoing than others. But for organizations of any appreciable size, all have to extend their personal reach by various means. For example, ethical hot lines and mail boxes can encourage organizational feedback. The employee survey is another means to obtain information about the ethical climate of an organization.

Many firms assign individual managers specific responsibility for directing or otherwise contributing to the firm's ethical program. (The corporate ombudsman position would be one example of a special contributor.) These people are well positioned to uncover ethical issues as well as new perspectives in thinking about ongoing concerns. As a result, they can play a vital role in helping senior managers to be more fully informed about ethical issues throughout the firm.

The board of directors has taken up the role of corporate conscience in many firms. This source of ethical guidance can be very effective in sensitizing management because of the peer relationships between its members and the most senior officers of the corporation and because of its latent power. At the same time, boards as a rule are still strongly shaped by the chief executive officer through his or her capacity to guide the selection of new board members, to make committee assignments, and, when holding the chair, to set the agenda.[14] As a result, senior executives can and do influence just how powerful a force for ethical behavior a board is to be.

Unintentional Sources

Not all actions affecting ethical sensitivity are done for that purpose. For example, the election of a union to represent the employees of Harvard University was bound to make the faculty and administration more sensitive to the ethical dimensions of the institution's personnel policies and practices. In some instances, managers might not even be aware of the effect that a particular action has or can have on ethical sensitivity. For example, the following comment by a middle-level research manager reveals the unintended and largely unrecognized positive impact that a recently sponsored quality improvement program was having on the way in which people treated each other in the company.

> The quality program has led to more and more openness and a greater willingness for people to talk about problems. Before, people were reluctant to speak out about problems because they were afraid to be branded as troublemakers or tattletales. Now it is okay to speak about quality-related problems because of the training we've had. This new attitude has spilled over to other considerations not necessarily connected to quality.

As a result of the quality program, employees are more able and more willing to speak out on a variety of ethical issues. From quality-related issues—such as What quality is a customer entitled to? What is it about the system that motivates employees to push through marginal or faulty products? Are suppliers being treated in a way to foster their best efforts?—it is only a short distance to broader concerns about the company's treatment of its customers, employees, suppliers, and other parties. In this situation, management appears unwittingly to have increased the organization's ability to be more sensitive to ethical issues and at the same time to have enabled the employees to be more active and possibly creative in their contributions to the firm's operations. It stands to reason that management ought to be far more effective in exploiting opportunities of this nature when it is aware of the interrelationships and acts on them than when it is oblivious to the possibilities.

One of the best ways for senior managers to tap into hidden as well as known sources of information is to let their interest in discussing ethical issues be known. In effect, if senior managers want to hear about ethical issues, they have to talk about them, as did John Dubinsky of Mark Twain Bancshares. The more clearly people throughout an organization know of this top management interest, the greater the quantity and quality of relevant information they are likely to communicate to it.[15] Only with open discussion of ethical issues can senior managers get the information and counsel they might need to gain a proper understanding of perplexing problems and determine the best course of action.

Managers' receptivity to the information they receive regarding ethical issues depends significantly, however, on the reason for their not knowing it. If their *not knowing* is merely a function of having been uninformed, then the information-gathering process described above, along with training in some cases, can correct the problem. But if the *not knowing* is the result of a desire, possibly not fully recognized, to avoid the personal discomfort and the costly complications that business ethics can cause, then simply gaining access to relevant information is not likely to be of much benefit. In such cases, management is likely to need help in learning how to deal with its defensive routines.[16]

Enhancing Judgment

Much of the information managers receive about ethical issues is confusing and highly charged in nature. Many actions called for can be costly or involve complex organizational changes. For these reasons, senior managers often turn to trusted associates for help in interpreting the significance of the information they receive and in considering the implications for policy and practice. This support structure can be *ad hoc* in its composition—a kind of personal kitchen cabinet—or it can include specific organizational units. The executive committee, typically comprising the firm's most senior officers, often plays this role. For Iverson at Nucor, it is the entire group of close to 50 senior managers who convene formally three times a year and otherwise interact on an ongoing basis. As Dubinsky's remarks early in the chapter reveal, outsiders can also provide a valuable forum for interpreting information and evaluating policy choices.

The point is not so much who should participate in such deliberations. Rather it is that business leaders need to give some thought as to how they might best draw help from people whose moral and managerial judgment they respect in interpreting information about ethical behavior and in considering the implications for company policy and practice.

Remaining Ethically Fit: An Ongoing Obligation

The shaping of senior management's ethical concerns obviously has to be an ongoing and dynamic process. Business context changes over time, and with it the kinds of ethical issues that arise and their relative importance. Moreover, ethical priorities and norms are moving targets.[17] For these reasons, business leaders must develop a capacity for continued learning and a willingness to reassess and revise their views in those situations where policies and practices fail to provide a morally acceptable outcome. When the changes are abrupt—such as those resulting from a radical change in corporate strategy or from a public awakening such as occurred with respect to sexual harassment during the Clarence Thomas Senate confirmation hearings for appointment to the United States Supreme Court—the signals for senior managers to re-examine their thinking on ethical policies and practices can be clear-cut. But when the changes are gradual, it may take a serious ethical failure or breakdown to alert management. A good case in point is the effect the Winan's affair had on Dow Jones & Company. In 1983, R. Foster Winan was indicted for alleged insider trading activities connected with his *Wall Street Journal* column, "Heard on the Street." A senior vice president explained the impact on the firm:

> In my thirty-three years with the company, the Winan affair was by far the most threatening of damaging the reputation of the firm of any I have known. We had an agonizing introspection following the disclosure. He was a hell of a good reporter. But were there signals that might have alerted us to this kind of behavior? Did we pay him enough? Was he checked out enough?
>
> This got us thinking about other things. Thirty years ago, this was a small organization. We really hadn't realized how large it had grown in recent years. The average employee tenure was only three years. In time we came to recognize the need to make employees aware of what this company stood for, to formalize a process that earlier had been informal.

The Dow Jones experience reveals the difficulty managers face in recognizing and responding to major changes that develop in the course of a gradual drift in circumstances. Internal relationships, attitudes, competitive pressures, and a host of other factors may change imperceptibly over time, like changes a young child experiences in growing up. And just as this child will outgrow its clothing, management will find its understanding of the ethical challenge it faces to be increasingly ill fitting over time.

Management's ability to uncover inadequacies in corporate ethical conduct clearly depends on its own knowledge and sensitivity. But it also depends on the organization's readiness to challenge management's thinking and actions. For this to happen, business leaders must succeed in tapping the powerful moral values that many of their people might have suppressed in their business lives. The organization needs to view business ethics as a positive experience that can provide satisfaction and fulfillment in its own right and not as a set of sanctions that constrain and threaten individuals in their jobs.

The companies most successful in achieving high standards of behavior are those in which senior management has consciously developed a sensitivity to and understanding of the ethical dimensions of their decisions. As a result, their values and ethical concerns are perceived throughout the organization as meaningful and sincere. While management's concerns alone will not ensure an organization's ethical performance—they have to be transformed into practice through the sound development of systems, procedures, and people—they do represent the critical starting point in giving direction and setting the right tone for the entire process of managing corporate ethics.

3

Going from Principles to Practice

To foster corporate ethics, top-level executives commonly take such actions as promulgating a code of ethics, offering information sessions and training programs, and expressing in words and by example their commitment to high standards of behavior. They might also assign one or more staff people responsibility for organizing and conducting a corporate ethics program. When done well, these and similar actions can contribute importantly to motivating corporate ethical behavior. But for this to happen, corporate leaders must do much more.

We can see this in normal business operations. Senior managers give inspirational talks, provide training, and assign staff responsibilities to gain organizational support of the corporation's business strategy, but they would never limit themselves to such efforts. Instead, they are likely to rely primarily on basic and powerful organizing and motivating mechanisms already in effect in the firm, such as reporting relationships, planning and control systems, and performance evaluation. Managing corporate ethics also requires the use of these core managerial processes.

The task for senior management is to establish a clear, cohesive, and comprehensive structure of policies and procedures that functions to promote ethical behavior in two complementary ways. It should foster an organization's concern for the rights and interests of all parties affected by the corporation. It should also provide safeguards to reduce or remove temptations. In the words of a 1940s Johnny Mercer hit song, the structure must "accentuate the positive, eliminate the negative." This chapter begins by examining how two companies, Lincoln Electric and General Mills, organize themselves to institutionalize ethical inducements and safeguards. It then looks at how the use of ethical codes can play a part in the process.

Management Systems Promoting Ethical Principles

This ability to weave ethical concerns into the basic managerial processes is generally evident in the ethical firms studied. Few enterprises, however, succeed in carrying out this assimilation more fully than does the Lincoln Electric Company, even though in the doing, senior management makes no explicit reference to corporate ethics as such. The Lincoln Electric story shows how senior management's concern for the valid interests of employees, customers, and shareholders can be built into the woof and warp of a company's operating structure.

The Lincoln Electric Company

For more than 40 years, The Lincoln Electric Company has been the world's largest manufacturer of arc welding products.[1] The company's leadership position reflects its continuing ability to outperform its competitors in productivity, product value, sales, and profits. The company's successful approach rested on both ethical commitment and sound strategy.

The starting point for Lincoln Electric's enduring business success was clearly stated by James F. Lincoln in 1941.

> It is the job of The Lincoln Electric Company to give its customers more and more of a better product at a lower and lower price. This will also make it possible for the company to give to the worker and the stockholder a higher and higher return.[2]

Over the years, he continued to call attention to the importance of dividing the returns from successful business operations among customers, workers, and owners.

> There is no hard and fast rule to cover this division, other than the following. The worker (which includes management), the cus-

tomer, the owner, and all those involved must be satisfied that they are properly recognized or they will not cooperate, and cooperation is essential to any and all successful applications of incentives.[3]

In this comment, we can see the interplay of concern for economic performance and respect for others. Clearly, Lincoln has successful enterprise in mind when he speaks about the need to gain the cooperation of customers, workers, and investors. In contrast, reference to the idea that these parties "must be satisfied that they are properly recognized"—when taken together with his belief in the dignity of all workers and in his company's mission to serve the customer—points to an ethical dimension.

It is not uncommon to hear companies tout the notion of benefiting customers, employees, and shareholders. Unlike many others, Lincoln has in place a comprehensive and cohesive set of policies and procedures to achieve these goals. We will examine this structure first with respect to the marketplace, then to the workplace, and finally in overview so as to bring out the important interconnections.

Customer Focus

Taking the customers' interests into account at Lincoln Electric focuses on providing the best value possible. To supply "more and more of a better product at a lower and lower price," the company competes on the basis of price, quality, product performance, service, and warranty.[4] The importance of these particular factors becomes clear from a brief examination of the arc welding business.

Arc welding, a process utilizing electric current to fuse various metals at a temperature of approximately 10,000° Fahrenheit, poses formidable technical challenges. The welding is often done under adverse conditions: weather can be inclement; joints not easily accessible; and schedules overbearing, putting pressure for hurried output. Even under ideal working conditions, the welding characteristics of specific metals can vary markedly, affecting the strength of the joint. Finally, the joint must hold under various stresses—mechanical, chemical, thermal, electrical—for long periods of time, often decades and more.

These conditions place a premium on product performance and quality. They also make technical services important. Notwithstanding these technical challenges, specialized products account for only a small portion of the arc welding business. With most products classed as standard commercial articles, low prices also become a key competitive factor.

Lincoln Electric's competitive strategy responds directly to these requirements. To set itself apart from other suppliers, the company emphasizes technical services. A former vice president of sales development characterized Lincoln's approach:

> Our approach to the customer is to go in and learn what he is doing and show him how to do it better. For many companies our people become their experts in welding. They go in and talk to a foreman. They might say, "Let me put on a headshield and show you what I'm talking about." That's how we sell them.[5]

He went on to explain how the company prepares its field salespeople to serve the customer in this manner:

> We start out with engineering graduates and put them through our seven-month training program. They learn how to weld, and we teach them everything we can about equipment, metallurgy, and design. Then they spend time on the rebuild line [where machines brought in from the field are rebuilt] and even spend time in the office seeing how orders are processed. Finally, before the trainees go out into the field, they have to go into our plant and find a better way of making something. Then they make a presentation to [the company's chairman], just as if he were one of our customers.[6]

Product quality and performance features are also important to this approach. John Weaver, who spent 26 years in domestic sales before being named vice president for international sales, makes this point, "I have always felt that I and my salespeople were really long-term consultants to our customers rather than peddlers. We try to stress what our product can do for the customer. It is comforting to know that we offer the best product and can sell it at the best value." Weaver's confidence in the product is justified by the widespread commitment in Lincoln to quality and honest dealings. This commitment was apparent in the comments from people throughout the organization, such as the following remark by John Velliky, vice president of engineering.

> The company follows the NEMA [National Electrical Manufacturers Association] and UL [Underwriters Laboratory] standards fully. Let's say a motor heats up to 120° Fahrenheit and the specification for maximum heat is 115°. Even if none of the customers would

know about it, so long as Lincoln Electric knows, it is not ac-ceptable.

A variety of policies are in place to foster an honest concern for the customer and safeguard against abuses. These policies, and, more important, their ethical purpose, are understood and accepted as indicated in the following remarks by various salespeople.

On commissions: To prevent unnecessary conflicts between our interests and those of our customers, we are on straight salary. No commissions.

On opportunities for kickbacks: Salespeople cannot negotiate price. Everything is sold on book price with no exceptions. Over time, Lincoln Electric has been so straight on this that pressure for special deals has ceased. This practice helps to discourage any one person from putting out his hand.

On gifts to customers and the possibility of payoffs: We bust our butts to serve the customer. Isn't that enough? Gift-giving just doesn't flow with the concept of this company.

Exhibit 3-1 shows how Lincoln Electric's policies and practices, taking the customers' interests into account, come together. For example, the first six entries on the list support the company's strategic objective of delivering high quality products to its cus-tomers as explained below.

1. Stringent quality control procedures at the plant ensure that only high quality products are delivered and help put a spot-light on manufacturing trouble spots.
2. Paying workers only for good output and requiring rework without compensation, coupled with the practice of quality control, motivate proper workmanship the first time.
3. Emphasizing standard consumables and equipment rather than special and custom products permits dedicated manu-facturing processes that can result in consistent high qual-ity. (Dedicated manufacturing can also result in lower costs and consequently lower prices.)
4. Backward integration (such as making its own electric mo-tors for the welding machines) helps to ensure quality by putting more of the company's products under its direct manufacturing control.
5. Close coordination between product design and manufactur-ing methods leads to simpler and more reliable products produced in an effective manner.

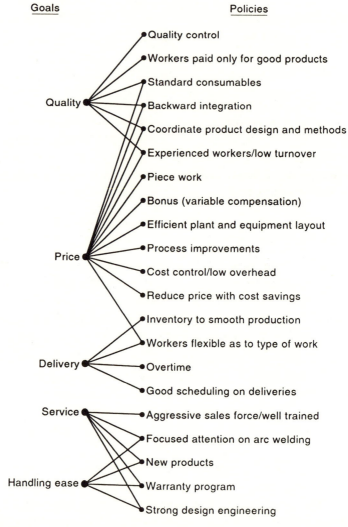

Goals Policies

- Quality control
- Workers paid only for good products
- Standard consumables
- Backward integration
- Coordinate product design and methods
- Experienced workers/low turnover
- Piece work
- Bonus (variable compensation)
- Efficient plant and equipment layout
- Process improvements
- Cost control/low overhead
- Reduce price with cost savings
- Inventory to smooth production
- Workers flexible as to type of work
- Overtime
- Good scheduling on deliveries
- Aggressive sales force/well trained
- Focused attention on arc welding
- New products
- Warranty program
- Strong design engineering

Quality
Price
Delivery
Service
Handling ease

Exhibit 3–1 Lincoln Electric's policies to help meet its goals for customers

6. The many policies (described below) that result in low worker turnover and high experience levels also contribute to high quality workmanship.

A similar analysis can be made for each of the other company objectives for serving its customers (e.g., eleven policies contribute to lower price, four to rapid delivery, etc.)

Lincoln Electric's success in the marketplace depends to a large degree on the productivity of its workforce. The company's policies and procedures are every bit as forceful in taking the workers' interests into account as they are regarding customers.

Employee Focus

James Lincoln believed in the existence of considerable latent abilities for most people, in the need to help people to develop these abilities, and in the powerful motivation that comes from having one's abilities and achievements recognized. The following excerpts from one of his writings on the subject give some idea on how he viewed industrial management.[7]

> There is all the difference imaginable between the grudging, distrustful, half-forced cooperation and the eager wholehearted vigorous cooperation of men working together for a common purpose.
>
> If those crying loudest about the inefficiencies of labor were put in the position of the wage earner, they would react as he does. The worker is not a man apart. He has the same needs, aspirations and reactions as the industrialist. A worker will not cooperate on any program that will penalize him. Does any manager?
>
> Higher efficiency means fewer man-hours to do a job. If the worker loses his job more quickly, he will oppose higher efficiency.
>
> Continuous employment of workers is essential to industrial efficiency. This is a management responsibility. Laying off workers during slack times is death to efficiency. The worker thrown out is a trained man. To replace him when business picks up will cost much more than the savings of wages during the layoff. Solution? The worker must have a guarantee that if he works properly his income will be continuous.
>
> The calling of the minister, the doctor, the lawyer, as well as the manager, contains incentive to excel. Excellence brings rewards, self-esteem, respect. Only the hourly worker has no reason to excel.

These views on taking the workers' interests into account are embodied in the company's operating policies and practices, notably with respect to compensation, job security, shared control of the work environment, and dignity.[8]

Compensation
Compensation policies are the key element of James F. Lincoln's philosophy of "incentive management." Lincoln Electric's compensation system has two components: wages based solely on piecework output for most factory jobs, and a year-end bonus that could

equal or exceed an individual's full annual regular pay. As indicated below, considerable care is taken to ensure proper functioning of this pay-for-performance scheme.

Almost all production workers at Lincoln are paid on a straight piecework plan. William Irrgang [chairman in 1975] explained this approach:

> Wherever practical, we use the piecework system. This system can be effective, and it can be destructive. The important part of the system is that it is completely fair to the worker. When we set a piecework price, that price cannot be changed just because, in management's opinion, the worker is making too much money. Whether he earns two times or three times his normal amount makes no difference. Piecework prices can only be changed when management has made a change in the method of doing that particular job and under no other conditions. If this is not carried out 100 percent, piecework cannot work.[9]

A time study department establishes piecework prices that are guaranteed by the company until methods are changed or a new process introduced. Employees can challenge the price if they believe it to be unfair. Employees are expected to guarantee their own quality and are not paid for defective work until it has been repaired on their own time.

The second element of the compensation system is a year-end bonus, which has been paid each year since 1934. As explained in the *Employee's Handbook*, "The bonus, paid at the discretion of the company, is not a gift, but rather it is the sharing of the results of efficient operation on the basis of the contribution of each person to the success of the company for that year." All employees are eligible to share in the bonus except the chairman and president. In 1992, the year-end incentive cash bonus totaled $48 million, an average of almost $18,000 for each of the company's 2,688 employees. (For comparison sake, cash dividends for shareholders were about $7.5 million.)

An individual's share of the bonus pool is determined by a semiannual "merit rating" that measures individual performance compared to that of other members of the department or work group. In determining an employee's merit rating, five factors are evaluated separately: dependability, quality, output, ideas, and cooperation.

Performance rating is undoubtedly a key area where the company's treatment of its workers comes under close scrutiny by its workforce. The seriousness with which performance appraisal is taken at Lincoln Electric is apparent in the following comment by a tool room supervisor.

> Merit ratings is the most difficult thing I have to do. I get sick for two weeks in May and again in November when I have to make decisions about performance and have to tell my people. If anyone is unhappy with my call, he can see my boss, or for that matter, go straight to the president. Over the past ten years, I've had individual workers challenge my rating three or four times. I was careful to document workers attendance and behavior so that my assessments were confirmed. But I've heard of others who have had their assessments overturned.

The company also provides employee retirement benefits based on length of service and job category. The following account reveals the extent to which employees are seen as entitled to these benefits:

> The company's retirement program includes full pay at age 65 for anyone who has been with the company 40 years. There has never been mandatory retirement. An employee who keeps working after 65 can receive his retirement check, his regular paycheck, and the year-end bonus as well.[10]

Job Security

Lincoln complements its rating and pay system with a Guaranteed Continuous Employment Plan. Under this plan, every full-time employee who has been with the company at least three years (two years until recently) is guaranteed employment for at least 75 percent of the standard 40-hour week.

The guarantee of employment is seen by the company as an essential element in the incentive plan. Without such a guarantee, according to management, employees would be more likely to resist improved production and efficiency for fear of losing their jobs. In accepting the guaranteed continuous employment plan, employees agree to perform any job assigned them and to work overtime during periods of high activity.

In line with job security, Lincoln Electric has a strict policy of filling all but entry level positions by promoting from within the company. Whenever an opening occurs, a notice is posted on the many bulletin boards located throughout the company's premises. Any interested employee can apply for an open position. Because of the company's sustained growth and policy of promoting from within, employees have substantial opportunities for advancement.

Shared Control of the Work Environment
James Lincoln recognized early the need to give voice to the workers if the company was to inspire "the eager wholehearted vigorous cooperation of men working together for a common purpose" that he favored. This prompted him in 1914 to create an Advisory Board comprising elected employee representatives from all parts of the organization. This board provides a forum in which employees can bring issues of concern to top management's attention, question company policies, and make suggestions for their improvement. As described in the *Employee's Handbook,*

> Board service is a privilege and responsibility of importance to the entire organization. In discussions or in reaching decisions, Board members must be guided by the best interests of the Company. These also serve the best interests of its workers. They should seek at all times to improve the cooperative attitude of all workers and see that all realize they have an important part in our final results.

All Advisory Board meetings are usually chaired by either the chairman or the president of Lincoln. Issues range widely, from conditions on the factory floor to various administrative procedures. Each is resolved on the spot or assigned to an executive for appropriate action. The seriousness of purpose is carefully conveyed to all employees. Minutes of the biweekly board meetings are posted on bulletin boards in each department and employee representatives explain the board's actions to the other workers in their department. The questions raised in the minutes of a given meeting are usually answered in the next set of minutes. This procedure, which has not changed significantly in 80 years, is a constant reminder of management's respect for employees' opinions and concerns. The direct involvement by the company's most senior executives in the meetings and their commitment to resolve the issues raised gives weight to this process as nothing else could.

Dignity
In James Lincoln's view, every person is entitled to be treated with dignity. Management's attention to compensation and job security and its responsiveness to employees' views are major expressions of this belief. Above and beyond these measures, Lincoln Electric also avoids perquisites of rank. Executive offices are plain and func-

tional. Parking is on a first-come, first-served basis.[11] Everyone eats in the company cafeteria, including visitors. Another means for aligning the interests and status of workers with those of managers is to encourage stock ownership. As a result of this effort, approximately half the employees are shareholders.

Employee Good Will
The employees' response to Lincoln Electric's long-standing efforts to provide them with high wages, job security, self-control, and dignity through its policies and procedures was clearly positive. (See Exhibit 3-2 for a list of explicit policies in support of these goals for employees.) In their in-depth study of the company, Fast and Berg reported "that employees generally liked working at Lincoln."[12] A subsequent independent examination of employees attitudes corroborated this assessment, noting their recognition of management's efforts "to be open, honest, and fair" with them.[13] The following account of how some factory workers reacted to a severe sales downturn in the early 1980s gives further evidence of their good will to the company (as well as testimony to their resilience and latent abilities).

> Two years ago, when the Lincoln Electric Company's sales were sagging because of the recession, 50 factory workers volunteered to help out.
> After a quick sales training course, they took to the road, their only compensation 18 1/2 cents a mile for expenses, with no money for lodging or meals. Their objective: to help sell the company's Model SP200, a small welder introduced a couple of years earlier for use in small machine shops and auto body shops.
> The tactic worked. People who had been plant workers all their lives walked into body shops all over the country and said: "Hi. I'm a factory worker from Lincoln Electric. I've got a welder I'd like to sell you." The pitch brought in $10 million in new sales and the small arc welder is now one of Lincoln's best-selling items.[14]

There were also misgivings to be sure. One supervisor complained about "the tremendous pressure from the top to perform." He went on to temper this criticism as follows: "Offsetting this pressure is the fact that the top managers are honest people. You know, it is harder to get discharged from Lincoln Electric than from almost any other company." This comment reveals a widespread perception among Lincoln Electric workers of being treated with decency and fairness. For many, pride in being tough and suc-

Goals

Policies

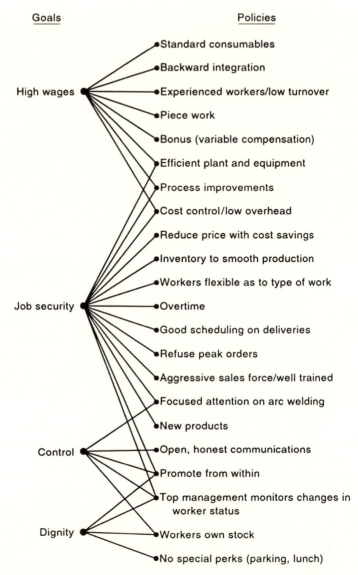

Exhibit 3–2 Lincoln Electric's policies to help meet its goals for employees

cessful competitors also helps to offset the pressures to perform. As Donald F. Hastings, Chairman and CEO of Lincoln Electric, observed in a network television interview in early 1992, "Good hard work never hurt anyone."

Integrating the Full Structure

Along with its structured efforts to treat customers and employees with respect, Lincoln Electric also has a set of policies to take investors' interests into account. For senior management, the challenge is not only to carry out the various policies for each of three important constituencies, but also to make them work in concert. An overview of how Lincoln Electric's policies and practices, individually and collectively, serve customers, employees, and investors is shown in Exhibit 3-3. This table highlights two points. First, many policies serve more than one corporate objective. For example, the workforces' flexibility with respect to the type of work a person will do in difficult times (item 14) helps to keep costs—and therefore prices—down. It also contributes to workers' job security by increasing an individual worker's usefulness as company needs change. And it helps the company meet tight delivery schedules where a redeployment of manpower could free a bottleneck in the process flow.

Second, in some cases, policies with a purpose of achieving one or more objectives work against one or more other objectives. For example, the reason for the company's policy to refuse some orders during peak demand periods is to limit the buildup of its workforce so that layoffs can be avoided when demand slackens in this cyclical business. This policy goes counter to the objective of serving customers with prompt deliveries. It is interesting to note that in the two instances of conflict identified in the table, the objective of employee job security takes precedence over customer goals. This choice says a great deal about the depth of Lincoln Electric's commitment to its employees' welfare, notwithstanding its strong orientation to customers and profits. The wisdom of this resolution is nicely captured in the following assessment by David Aycock, former president of Nucor: "If you want to put customers first, you have to put employees first. It just stands to reason. If you don't have employees who feel good about their company, who will take care of customers?"

Aycock's down-to-earth perspective of the matter raises an interesting question about the Lincoln Electric story. One can ask, "What does all this have to do with corporate ethics? The company's approach is just good business practice." That is just the point. Most sound business practices—such as those that Tom Peters and Robert Waterman extolled in their bestseller *In Search of Excellence*—are also morally sound. Many of the policies and prac-

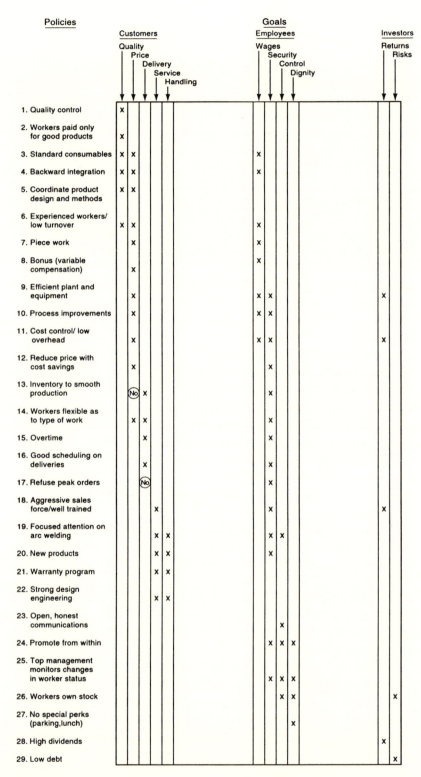

Exhibit 3–3 Lincoln Electric's policy structure to meet goals for customers, employees, and investors

tices described clearly reflect consideration and respect for individuals. Just because they make good business sense does not necessarily make them any less ethical. Interestingly, James Lincoln does not refer to "ethics" in his writings. Instead, he calls attention to what customers want and deserve, what workers want and deserve, and why anyone in these positions would want and deserve to be so treated. The management principles he espouses clearly embody ethical principles. As a result, ethical behavior permeates the company's style.

Ethical Safeguards

Human nature being what it is, people in authority have long recognized the limits of positive inducements and the need for preventive measures. In business, preventive measures range from senior management threatening punishment for unethical conduct to it taking actions that distance the organization from compromising situations or corrupting influences. As an example, we saw earlier how the Dover Corporation was prepared to reject the acquisition of a parking meter firm if that business would expose its people to unethical practices. Similarly, some companies stay out of certain countries because of the pressures their people are likely to experience with respect to bribes and other corrupt practices.

Of particular interest are the organizational mechanisms that ethical firms employ to counter pressures and temptations that are inherent and unavoidable in the normal course of business activities. Control systems and audits serve this purpose to some extent. However, they suffer the disadvantages of being external to the actions in question and largely after the fact. What is desirable is to have procedures and structures in place that discourage or prevent misconduct at the time decisions are made and actions taken. Every company that requires two authorizing signatures on large checks is practicing this concept. Along with such simple measures, managers can devise more elaborate organizational arrangements to provide important checks and balances.

The following account describes how General Mills dissuades its strongly driven product managers from resorting to false advertising in order to increase sales. It illustrates how organizational checks and balances can be carefully structured to guard against a major vulnerability.

General Mills

As a manufacturer of processed foods and breakfast cereals, General Mills depends heavily on promotion to win sales in a highly competitive business. Advertising, packaging, and point-of-sales promotion materials have to be eye-catching and appealing to a consumer who must choose from a profusion of competing brands also striving for attention, sometimes with extravagant claims.

To deal with this marketing challenge, product managers and marketing people are under considerable pressure to be innovative and aggressive in gaining consumer favor. One such manager, in commenting on the trade-off between profits and ethics, remarked, "General Mills prides itself on being an ethical company. Ultimately, however, we are evaluated on the numbers." The company's commitment to financial results is explicitly noted in its Statement of Corporate Values, "and the reliability to deliver promised results are all part of our commitment to each other, to our shareholders, and to our pride in 'The Company of Champions.' Our basic commitment to our shareholders is to deliver financial results that place us in the top quartile of all major companies." The pressure is also self-generated in that the high-energy, talented people responsible for individual products are driven by the very challenge of the competitive battle.

These pressures motivate product line managers to make the most compelling product claims possible to consumers. A blatantly dishonest assertion would not be tolerated; the General Mills legal department would put a stop to it if it were ever to go that far. But the line between right and wrong is not always clear in these matters. Dubious industry practices can project a false standard, especially for the brand manager intent on increasing or protecting market share. Moreover, it is not always easy to distinguish between artful truth and deceit. A senior executive gave some idea of this difficulty in connection with market research, "While there usually is no intention to cheat, people tend to view the data in the most optimistic way possible. They are often dealing with various shades of gray where judgement plays an important role."

Rather than remove pressures for economic performance—and risk suppressing the aggressive creativity of its product champions—General Mills employs organizational safeguards to protect against any improper or unethical practices, especially those having to do with product claims.

- One such safeguard is the review process for clearing advertising claims and nutritional labeling. Rita Warren, manager of technical services and nutrition education, describes her work:

> The question is whether the claims are truthful and whether they represent useful information to the consumer. There is always pressure to stretch the truth a little bit and make the product seem as positive as possible. What makes it tricky is that there are times when such requests are justified. For example, we agreed to add information on saturated fat, even though it was not required by law, because it offered consumers information they wanted.
>
> The biggest problem is when to sign off in the face of incomplete data. When there is a change in formulation, there is a need to test the product, to substantiate that the manufacturing process will be reliable in producing quality, and finally to monitor output. This takes time. The product line people, however, are under pressure to move quickly so as to get the new product out in the marketplace. Ultimately, I have to judge how much I am willing to anticipate the results.

- Another safeguard against improper product claims is provided by a centralized marketing service division. The following account by David Murphy, vice president and general manager of this division, illustrates the challenge of balancing responsible behavior and economic performance in a highly charged, complex organization like General Mills.

> Not long ago, a nutritionist began to raise questions about the way calcium was being used to promote a cereal. By advertising calcium on the box, we implied that this would help the consumer with respect to his or her calcium needs. The problem was that no one really knew how much of the calcium in the cereal would be bio-available. There was a general feeling that it was available to the body, but this was not proven.
>
> While there was no legal requirement to act on this issue and while many of our competitors were also touting calcium, I finally decided to push for a test confirming the bio-availability of calcium. This looked like a no-win situation on the surface. If the test proved positive, the company would simply continue doing what it already was doing. If it came out negative, the company would have to discontinue the claims until it could find another way of introducing calcium that would be bio-available. In either event, limited research resources would be tied up on this testing rather than on some other more positive quest. Moreover, the operating unit would not pay for

the testing. I felt, however, that we owed it to ourselves and to our customers and funded the testing from my budget.[15]

• Still another safeguard is the establishment of a unit that has responsibility for representing the consumers' point of view to those engaged in formulating and promoting food products.[16] The lengths to which General Mills goes to avoid misleading consumers is evident from the following description by Marsha Copeland of her duties as director of the Betty Crocker Food and Publications Center.

Among its various duties, my department represents the consumer to the company laboratories, oversees food preparation for commercials and cookbooks, and writes package cooking instructions. With respect to representing the consumer to the laboratories, we tell the technical people such things as the kinds of consumer utensils commonly in use. For example, while the product might cook best in a seven-by-seven inch cookie dish, it cannot be used for testing or for demonstrations since people do not normally have that size. In this connection, the department is concerned with how a product comes out when there are imperfect measures or when the heat and time are not exactly according to specifications. For this purpose, random tolerance tests are made starting with a base case where everything is done perfectly and then deviating with respect to the amount of water added, or the amount of heat, or how long it is cooked, etc., to see within what range the product will still come out properly. If the product fails too easily, it then has to be reformulated. Of course, we have to take into account the trade-off between increasing quality and what a consumer will be willing to pay.

For food commercials, our job is to make sure that the operating people or the photographers do not show food in some exaggeratedly favorable manner. For example, they might try to put more cake frosting on a cake than could be obtained from the portion normally sold to make it look better. This is not allowed. Similarly, potato souffles are not allowed to be shown filled to the top because that is not the way they can actually be cooked. The souffle tends to rise and then settle back. If you start with a small dish full, it would overflow into the oven. In a larger dish, it would settle down and be well below the rim. Obviously, the advertiser prefers to show a full dish because it looks more attractive.

When it comes to package instructions, the company is particularly concerned with safety. It is difficult to know what a consumer already knows and how well they can read. This can be a problem when young children use microwave products.

The General Mills approach of pushing product line managers to compete aggressively and of using corporate staff units to guard against illegal or otherwise unacceptable actions is common practice in large American companies. However, the elaborateness of the checks and balances and the seriousness with which these control functions are taken by most people in General Mills are exceptional. The successful working of this structured safeguard no doubt reflects in part General Mills' overall commitment to high ethical standards. However, two other considerations have an important direct bearing on why these safeguards command management's attention. One is the high likelihood of misconduct. For General Mills, the pressure for consumer attention—where products live and die on their market share—is intense. Given the nature of product advertising, standards of rightness can easily erode. The other factor is that the damages resulting from misconduct are likely to be high. False advertising can be costly both in its impact on business performance and on people's trust in management's integrity. Where risks are high, senior management has to go beyond good intentions and broad guidelines. Strong safeguards have to be in place to contain competitive moves within acceptable limits.

The use of safeguards is not without its costs. Devising, activating, and enforcing a protective measure takes valuable time and resources. Moreover, morale can be lowered when constraints are perceived as excessive or misguided. For these reasons, senior managers need to be somewhat selective in structuring safeguards. Top priority should be given to situations where temptation is high, where detection is difficult, and where the potential damage to the organization is high.

Formal Guidelines: Ethical Codes

In recent years, many businesses have come to rely on ethical codes of one sort or another to serve as the principal vehicle for articulating senior management's philosophy and expectations concerning the company's ethical conduct. By one account, over 80 percent of major corporations have adopted codes of ethics.[17] In many cases, management's expectations as to the role such codes can play in practice are unrealistically high. Normally, an ethical code provides an organization with a frame of reference, defining the areas of ethical concerns and the core values that are to guide

Cray people trust each other to do their jobs well and with the highest ethical standards.
— The Cray Style

What do high ethical standards mean in terms of business conduct? They mean that every practical decision is an ethical decision. Cray Research cannot and would not tell us how to conduct ourselves. For that, good judgement is necessary, and good judgement has no substitute. There exists, however, one simple test of our own judgement and ethical standards that applies to all situations and all decisions we make on behalf of Cray Research.

That test includes two basic questions:

How would I feel if my family and friends heard about my actions? Would I want an account of my activities to appear on the front page of the daily newspaper?

Test yourself. Cray's reputation and your own are at stake.

Exhibit 3–4 Ethics at Cray

action. At best, it can also be highly inspirational, inducing employees' pride and outsiders' admiration. What is important to understand is that ethical codes are just one of many managerial tools for motivating corporate ethical behavior . . . and generally not the most important.

Ethical codes vary widely in their purpose and content. Mark Twain Bancshares issues to its employees a 19-page, single-spaced typewritten document, titled "Ethical Standards and Conflict of Interest Policy," that instructs employees as to what is and what is not permissible conduct both in concept and in detail. In contrast, Cray Research's statement of ethics, shown in Exhibit 3-4, lays out a broad perspective in just 120 words. These dissimilar approaches reflect differences in the nature of the two businesses and of the two organizations.

Mark Twain, a bank operating out of multiple locations, deals with outside parties through many people in a business where improprieties tend to recur in connection with readily identifiable actions—such as political contributions, the exchange of gifts, and other acts of reciprocity. In this situation, management sees a need to ensure that everyone clearly understands where ethical problems are likely to arise and how to avoid them. Moreover, the use of detailed rules is in keeping with customary banking practices reflecting detailed state and federal regulations. At Cray Research, the potential ethical trouble spots are not so apparent for the business of selling supercomputers to sophisticated buyers. The broad statement of principles and lack of detailed instructions is also in keeping with management's emphasis on maintaining a creative and trusting environment for its professional employees. Clearly, the challenges senior managers face in these two companies differ, and the purpose and form of the documents differ accordingly.

The codes of most firms fall somewhere between Mark Twain Bancshares and Cray Research concerning detail and content. The more detailed codes would generally prescribe behavior for areas of special ethical concern, as illustrated by Dow Jones & Company in addressing conflicts of interest. An opening paragraph, with veiled reference to the painful Winan affair, forcefully sets the tone.

> It is important for all employees to keep in mind the tremendous embarrassment and damage to the Company's reputation and that of fellow employees that could come about through a lapse in judgment by one person, or someone closely associated with that person, no matter how well-intended that person may be. Because we think it is so essential that every employee be above suspicion, we consider any slip in judgment in the areas covered in this policy statement to be serious enough to warrant dismissal.

As can be seen from the following excerpts, the policy statement includes both broad and specific guidelines.

> We reiterate that it is not enough to be incorruptible and act with honest motives. It is equally important to use good judgment and conduct one's outside activities so that no one—management, our editors, a SEC investigator, or a political critic of the Company—has any grounds for even raising the suspicion that an employee misused a position with the Company.
>
> • • •
>
> (ii) No employee regularly assigned to a specific industry should invest, nor should his family, in any company engaged in whole or significant part in that industry.

(iii) No employee with knowledge of a forthcoming article, item or advertisement concerning a company or industry should, prior to the publication of such article, item or advertisement, invest or in any way encourage or assist any other person in investing in that company or companies in that industry; nor should the employee sell or assist any other person in selling a security in that company prior to publication without the approval of the appropriate Management Committee member.[18]

Focused guidelines of this nature obviously should help people to become more sensitive to the issues in question and more knowledgeable about how to behave. What is more important, their impact can easily extend beyond the specific items covered as employees project the spirit and rules of behavior to situations that are only marginally related or even totally unrelated to those addressed.

These benefits are not realized in many companies for a variety of reasons. Some codes are mere window dressing. They are meant to look good but not to interfere with the realities of the business. The hypocrisy, readily apparent to those most closely involved with the firm's business operations, simply makes a mockery of the process. Many codes—and these can be found in highly reputable, major firms—fail because of their self-serving nature. They focus on employee compliance with regulations intended to protect the company, giving little regard to the firm's obligations to its people or to other parties. According to one study, most codes "are either paternalistic or authoritarian in tone, telling employees in effect that ethical expertise is correlated positively with salary and status,"[19] A comprehensive commentary on codes of ethics reports that only 40 out of the 155 codes studied incorporate declarations of company obligations to employees. It argues that the inclusion of information about rights and privileges of employees in an ethical code is more likely to inspire faith and obedience to the code on the part of the employees than its neglect.[20] But even codes that are well intended and well structured can fail to be taken seriously.

Ensuring Credibility

Ethical codes, especially those that are less detailed and strive to inspire (so-called credos), by their very nature risk being perceived as little more than managerial rhetoric, high-sounding words empty of substance. Senior managers cannot simply produce and publish an ethical code. They also must take actions that help dispel any skepticism that such statements tend to evoke.

The credibility an organization accords a new code or credo depends on several factors. The quality of the statement is obviously important. It needs to be well drafted and bear relevance to the corporation's needs. Also critical is senior managers' commitment to the individual precepts as well as to the overall spirit of the statement. The more deeply involved they are in conceptualizing and drafting the statement, the more positive they are likely to be in this regard. Third is how effectively they are able to convey the importance and relevance of the statement to the organization at large. Fourth is the extent to which subordinates are made accountable for its observance.

The introduction of a new code or credo is not the only occasion when credibility is at issue. Credibility can be lost over time. This happened at Johnson & Johnson. How management dealt with this problem is broadly instructive, touching on each of the four factors listed above.

Johnson & Johnson Credo
Robert Wood Johnson, "the General," son of the founder and chairman of J&J from 1938 to 1963, was generally credited as the individual most responsible for shaping the company's character. His views, formalized in the 1940s as the company's Credo, underscored the company's responsibilities to its customers, to its employees, to the communities in which it operated, and finally to its stockholders. (The most recent version is shown in Exhibit 3-5.) For years, it was generally acknowledged as providing an underlying and unifying philosophy guiding all important decisions. The Credo was prominently displayed in every manager's office.

During the late 1970s, Jim Burke, then the company's president and soon to become chief executive officer and chairman of the board, perceived a growing tokenism in the organization's commitment to the Credo. He described his efforts to revitalize people's awareness of the relevance and importance of this statement:

> People like my predecessor believed the Credo with a passion, but the operating unit managers were not universally committed to it. There seemed to be a growing attitude that it was there but that nobody had to do anything about it. So I called a meeting of some 20 key executives and challenged them. I said, "Here's the Credo. If we're not going to live by it, let's tear it off the wall. If you want to

Our Credo

We believe our first responsibility is to the doctors, nurses and patients,
to mothers and fathers and all others who use our products and services.
In meeting their needs everything we do must be of high quality.
We must constantly strive to reduce our costs
in order to maintain reasonable prices.
Customers' orders must be serviced promptly and accurately.
Our suppliers and distributors must have an opportunity
to make a fair profit.

We are responsible to our employees,
the men and women who work with us throughout the world.
Everyone must be considered as an individual.
We must respect their dignity and recognize their merit.
They must have a sense of security in their jobs.
Compensation must be fair and adequate,
and working conditions clean, orderly and safe.
We must be mindful of ways to help our employees fulfill
their family responsibilities.
Employees must feel free to make suggestions and complaints.
There must be equal opportunity for employment, development
and advancement for those qualified.
We must provide competent management,
and their actions must be just and ethical.

We are responsible to the communities in which we live and work
and to the world community as well.
We must be good citizens — support good works and charities
and bear our fair share of taxes.
We must encourage civic improvements and better health and education.
We must maintain in good order
the property we are privileged to use,
protecting the environment and natural resources.

Our final responsibility is to our stockholders.
Business must make a sound profit.
We must experiment with new ideas.
Research must be carried on, innovative programs developed
and mistakes paid for.
New equipment must be purchased, new facilities provided
and new products launched.
Reserves must be created to provide for adverse times.
When we operate according to these principles,
the stockholders should realize a fair return.

Johnson & Johnson

Exhibit 3–5 Johnson & Johnson *Our Credo*

change it, tell us how to change it. We either ought to commit to it
or get rid of it."

The meeting was a turn-on, because we were challenging people's own personal values. Every word got attention. As a result it
forced people to think about what business was all about and what
they were all about and whether or not they could live with the
principles which we espouse. By the end of the session, the managers

had gained a great deal of understanding about, and enthusiasm for, the beliefs in the Credo. Subsequently, Dave Clare [J&J's president and chief operating officer] and I have met with small groups of J&J managers all over the world to challenge the Credo.

In this effort to regain organizational commitment to the Credo, Burke attended to each of the factors affecting credibility. One, the Credo was examined and challenged word by word to reassure its relevance and quality. As a result, several modifications were made to adapt the statement to changed circumstances. Two, the initial challenge meeting provided senior managers with an opportunity to redefine the relevance and importance of the guidelines and rekindle their enthusiasm for the Credo. Three, the year-long series of meetings that Burke and Clare held with small groups of J&J people throughout the world was a major effort to convey the Credo's relevance and importance to the organization as a whole. Four, senior managers held their subordinates accountable for the Credo's observance by employing its precepts as standards for evaluating decisions and actions. The following account illustrates this last factor.

> . . . when a company manager suggested closing down an older unprofitable plant in a small southern town in the United States, the executive committee had a long discussion with him about possible alternatives and the responsibilities which they felt J&J had to the people in that town. They altered the plan substantially, suggested to another J&J company which was seeking to expand that it use part of the old facility and some of the employees. Two hundred jobs were retained as a result. The committee also altered the severance and relocation programs which the company manager had recommended and helped set up a local recruiting service for the industries in that region. At no time was the company manager's judgment about closing an unprofitable business in question, but the executive committee broadened the balance of his plan to bring it more into line with the way in which the Credo describes treating employees and communities. It also expected him to learn from this experience.[21]

For Burke, the strongest evidence of the Credo's power was in the company's response to the Tylenol crisis.[22]

> I do not think that we could have done what we did with Tylenol if we hadn't all gone through the process of challenging ourselves and committing ourselves to the Credo. We had dozens of people making hundreds of decisions and all on the fly. And they

had to make them as wisely as they knew how. The reason they made them as well as they did is they knew what the set of beliefs that the institution they worked for were, so they made them based on that set of beliefs. We made very, very few mistakes.

I think that the Tylenol story is the most powerful thing that has occurred in American business to underline the value of a moral statement.

The power of J&J's Credo to guide and motivate behavior does not come from the words—even Burke admits that they sound pretentious in today's setting—but from the validity of the concepts and senior management's abilities to inspire organizational commitment to their enactment.

Subsequently, J&J initiated a Credo survey program that asked employees to rate in a detailed, confidential questionnaire how well the company, its management, and their immediate supervisors were meeting the principal responsibilities defined in the Credo. It is important to note how management used the survey to bolster its ethical sensitivity where the need was greatest. According to one observer's remarks about the survey, "The document is heavily weighted toward J&J's responsibility toward employees. This is partly due to its being an employee (as opposed to, say, a customer) survey, and partly due to the fact that for a long time Jim Burke had the sense that employee responsibility was probably the weakest area of Credo performance for the company."[23] It would seem natural and obvious for managers committed to ethical behavior to focus attention on their ethical blind spots and their less well-developed areas of ethical concern. That so few do is a tribute to Burke's understanding of what needs to be done to advance a firm's ethical standards and to his courage in running the risk of opening a Pandora's Box of nettlesome ethical dilemmas and challenges.

Ethical codes rarely play so powerful a role as witnessed in J&J. A more usual experience is likely to be that reported by a committee of senior executives at Armstrong World Industries in evaluating the content and role of the company's statement of ethical principles.

Our impression is that the conduct of our employees is one of the significant strengths of our company, and that we should protect and nurture that strength. It is difficult, however, to relate that strength to the existence of our Operating Principles. . . . The role of the Operating Principles seems to have been one of passive presence. They exist, they are accepted as being appropriate, they are the source of some pride and comfort, and they are occasionally quoted (though sometimes to support widely divergent views). That is probably about as much as we should expect from them. Operating Principles, by whatever name you choose to call them, cannot create and maintain a strong moral and ethical climate, but they can reinforce that climate.

As the report indicates, an ethical code is just one element of many for motivating moral business behavior. The conclusion that the primary role of an ethical code is to reinforce, rather than to create, a strong moral and ethical climate clearly challenges the common practice of using such standards and guidelines as a centerpiece of a corporate ethics program. The credibility and value of such codes depends on what other steps senior management takes to foster ethical behavior, especially with the key organizational processes that guide decision making and action.

An Ethically Predisposing Structure of Policies and Procedures

The experiences of Lincoln Electric, General Mills, and J&J are instructive in several ways.[24] Perhaps the most important lesson for senior managers has to do with just recognizing the vital role a comprehensive and cohesive structure of policies and practices can play in applying and extending their ethical aspirations throughout an organization. Such a policy structure contributes to the moral health of a firm by motivating the morally indecisive person to behave ethically—and not to behave unethically—and by providing confirmation and comfort to the ethically minded.

The accounts in this chapter also indicate the need for such policy structures to give special attention to activities that are both critical to business results and open to abuse. Product claims is such an area for General Mills; for Lincoln Electric, it is protecting employee interests in the face of the powerful demands from customers and investors. Such areas for concern can be different for individual business units in a corporation and can change over time as conditions and objectives change. Where expectations and pressures for performance are high, policies and practices in support of ethical behavior need to be commensurately powerful.

One place for most senior managers to look for possible problems with expectations and motivational pressures is in connection with a firm's reward system. Compensation policies and practices can be critical determinants of organizational behavior and therefore have an important bearing on corporate ethics. The growing emphasis on pay-for-performance intensifies this connection. To the extent that the performance measures are narrowly focused on profits, they are capable of exerting strong pressures on managers and workers to take whatever actions that are deemed necessary to achieve bottom-line targets.[25] Moreover, as the National Commission on Fraudulent Financial Reporting concluded, rewarding managers who engage in manipulative practices for achieving their budget targets is likely to degrade a firm's financial reporting practices.[26]

The need for senior managers to define performance in "pay-for-performance" as being more than just profits (or other financial returns, market share, etc.) to include ethical performance should be obvious. What is likely to be less obvious is how difficult it can be to do so in a way that creates an effective countervailing force to profit pressures. An in-depth study of twelve corporations explains why profits can be so potent and pervasive as a motivating force in today's business organization. It states that almost without exception, corporate managers place their primary emphasis on the accounting profit measures because they prefer to evaluate their subordinates on the same terms on which they and the corporation are being evaluated. The measures are relatively precise and objective because they are based on an elaborate set of measurement rules, and they are audited in some detail on a periodic basis. And most managers understand the measures because they have been working with them for all of their professional careers.[27]

The measurement and evaluation of ethical behavior suffers by comparison. Instead of the precise and objective quantitative scale that profits offer, the measure of ethical behavior depends on qualitative assessments, often involving a great deal of subjectivity. In general, profits of $3 million are half again as good as profits of $2 million. Similarly, a loss of $200,000 is worse than to break even. But how does one compare the gravity of selling adulterated products versus dumping dangerous wastes into a river or against allowing a possible safety hazard in a factory to persist?

Moreover, while profits and losses are equally visible, positive ethical actions (corresponding to profits) tend to be less noticeable in most companies than comparable ethical breaches (somewhat akin to financial losses). Countless individual decisions to do what is right in the course of business operations are taken for granted and go unnoticed. Many, if not most, of these ethical decisions are made on a mental auto-pilot, with little or no explicit consideration given to taking advantage of others. And so, while profits from routine operations count as much as those from extraordinary actions, the bulk of positive ethical behavior is largely unmeasured, and probably immeasurable.

The problem of incentives generating unintended consequences that undermine senior management's intentions is not limited to compensation schemes. Any strong pressures for motivating behavior and performance—even when intended for some ethical purpose—runs the risk of unintended consequences. For example, a resolute dedication to serving customers could result in excessive demands on employees or suppliers. The broad challenge in managing a structure of policies and practices that are supposed to motivate ethical behavior is to ensure its continuing strength and vitality while guarding against undesirable consequences.

4

Reinforcing the Ethical Charge

The job of managing corporate ethics is never quite finished. As William Adams, chairman and president of Armstrong World Industries observed, "A company's ethical conduct is something like a big flywheel. It might have a lot of momentum, but it will eventually slow down and stop unless you add energy." With this simile, Adams points to the importance of senior managers continuing their active efforts to reinforce and nurture organizational commitment to ethical practices, even in firms with strong ethical traditions.

This chapter looks at how companies with strongly established ethical values maintain organizational commitment (prevent the ethical flywheel from slowing down). It describes some of the many different ways in which senior managers can reinforce a firm's formal structure of ethically related policies and procedures. While most of these reinforcing activities are likely to be employed by almost any firm promoting business ethics, the relative emphasis given to each, as well as how each is integrated into a cohesive whole, differs from company to company. A comparison of two companies shows how senior managers take into account the distinctive character of their company and the particular business situation it faces in shaping an overall approach. At Armstrong World Industries, a conventional industrial firm operating in mature and highly competitive markets, emphasis is placed on making the rules clear, checking performance, and punishing violations. Hewlett-Packard, competing in high technology electronics, emphasizes quite different activities in its efforts to reinforce ethical standards that are similar to those at Armstrong. Finally, with General Mills, we examine corporate involvement in community service to consider how such activities relate to ethical behavior.

Armstrong World Industries

Armstrong World Industries has a long history of ethical concern. At the time of its founding as a cork product manufacturer in 1860, just prior to the Civil War, business generally worked on the principle *Caveat Emptor* ("Let the buyer beware"). According to a published company history, Thomas Armstrong adopted the motto "Let the buyer have faith," and beginning in 1864, put his name on every bag of corks, making it one of the first products not sold directly to consumers to carry a manufacturer's brand.[1] By 1993, Armstrong World Industries was a major manufacturer of floor coverings, building products, furniture, and industrial products with total sales in excess of $2 billion. The company, with headquarters and major facilities in Lancaster, Pennsylvania, employed approximately 22,000 people and had plants in 17 states and 10 foreign countries.

Notwithstanding the company's size and complexity, and the strong competitive challenges it faces, the legacy of earning people's respect clearly continues to permeate the Armstrong organization. When asked how Armstrong sustains its ethical climate, Adams responded,

> We reinforce our commitment to ethical practice in several ways. First, we talk about ethics all the time. Second, the company has an explicit statement of principles to guide us in our actions. Third, we make sure to check on performance. Fourth, we punish the violators. Fifth, we give all our people the opportunity to talk to anyone in the company in connection with concerns about ethical issues. Access to the top people can be very important.

Other managers added to Adams's list, mentioning the kind of people hired, the continuity of values in the leadership of successive presiding officers, and deliberate efforts to remove temptations.

This list of factors, to which still others could be added, can be confusing to someone trying to understand how Armstrong management keeps the ethical flywheel turning. Grouping the various elements under two broad themes—promoting the company's ethical standards and discouraging misconduct—helps to reveal the overall coherence of Armstrong's reinforcing efforts.

Promoting Ethical Standards

Armstrong's statement of principles, shown in Exhibit 4-1, declares its commitment to business ethics. A great deal of senior management effort goes into reinforcing this declaration of intent in a variety of positive ways. The top-down character of its approach is shaped by such activities as ethical pep talks by the CEO and other senior managers, the skillful creation and use of inspirational stories, setting good examples through solicitous treatment of employees, and encouraging employees to turn to top management for guidance.

Ethical Pep Talks

Bill Adams plays a key role in sustaining the ethical tone that Armstrong achieved over the years. A recently hired technical manager gave some evidence of this when he said, "One of the things that struck me when I first joined Armstrong was the forceful talk about business ethics that Bill Adams gave at the orientation program. It made clear what is acceptable and what is not in

We firmly believe that the most significant factor contributing to our Company's progress has been the strict adherence to sound principles—principles laid down by the founder and carried forward and given new dimensions by succeeding managements.

PRINCIPLES

1. To respect the dignity and inherent rights of the individual human being in all dealings with people.

2. To maintain high moral and ethical standards and to reflect honesty, integrity, reliability and forthrightness in all relationships.

3. To reflect the tenets of good taste and common courtesy in all attitudes, words and deeds.

4. To serve fairly and in proper balance the interests of all groups associated with the business—customers, stockholders, employees, suppliers, community neighbors, government and the general public.

Exhibit 4–1 Armstrong World Industries operating principles

this company." Adams himself gives considerable weight to these sessions.

> One of my primary functions is to promote the company's values and culture. I am particularly concerned in getting new employees to understand these things. I feel it is important that I be the one to talk about our guiding principles, not the legal department or personnel.
>
> I have had people come up to me after being two days with us saying that they are relieved to hear that this is really the kind of company that they thought it would be. These people see themselves as naive and vulnerable and find it very reassuring when the president of the company reconfirms that this is a straight company that wants to do the right thing.

Other senior Armstrong managers are also active in setting this tone for new employees reporting to them.

Inspirational Stories

Company lore at Armstrong is replete with stories about how Tom Armstrong and his successors acted with concern for honest business dealings. An early legend concerns a salesman who boasted about selling, at a price of forty cents a gross, a large lot of odd-sized corks that had been hard to move. Tom Armstrong, who knew the proper price to be only thirty cents, made the salesman go back to the customer, say that a mistake had been made in the quotation and that the corks would be billed at thirty cents.[2] Eighty years later, this legendary episode was magnified when Armstrong determined that it was making too much profit on its subcontract to an aircraft manufacturer during World War II. As the story goes, a $500,000 refund check was sent one month and another check the next to a surprised customer.[3]

From the legends of Tom Armstrong and the early leaders of the company to accounts of recent and contemporaneous occurrences, stories provide Armstrong managers with a powerful means of defining and encouraging ethical behavior. It was not unusual in the course of interviews connected with this study for managers to illustrate their comments about Armstrong's ethical standards with stories. The following narration by a senior manager was typical.

> When Ralph Williams, a Lancaster quality assurance manager, discovered that one of the carpets being sold by a recently acquired company was flammable, he insisted that it be recalled from the

trade and that any carpets already installed be replaced without charge. The operating managers were aghast at this directive and practically refused to speak to him. When Joe Jones [Armstrong's president 1983–1987] next visited the carpet plant, he called a meeting of the whole top management and said, "I've heard what Ralph Williams has done. If anyone here doesn't agree with that kind of action, it is probably time for that person to resign."

This single account speaks volumes about how strongly Armstrong senior managers feel about corporate ethical behavior.

The strong family tradition found in Armstrong lends itself to the creation and telling of stories. In this setting, managers are conscious of the example they must set and are skillful in preserving these examples as stories for their instructional and inspirational value.

Setting Good Examples

The speeches and stories would not count for much over time without supporting actions. In few respects do the aphorisms "Actions speak louder than words" and "Practice what you preach" apply more forcefully than to business ethics. The credibility of senior management's ethical intentions rests firmly on how it behaves, and, from the workers' point of view, on how it treats them.

Armstrong senior managers are well aware of this connection and openly acknowledge their function as role models. The impressions they might give concerning ethical standards are an important consideration in deciding to act one way or another. Their efforts to show employees respect and to set good examples are evident in the organization. Employees at all levels reported actions affecting themselves and others that helped them to feel good about the company and to trust management at its word. The remarks of Linda Baldwin, a word processing secretary in the Consumers Affair Department, give some idea of how senior management is seen to apply Armstrong's lofty operating principles at lower levels in the organization.

> This is a good place to work, especially as a black female. I love my job. One reason is that they trust you.
>
> We have to deal with customers who are often angry and upset. Our department has a lot of staff meetings to instruct us on how to behave. Our vice president actually returns calls to customers. This blew my mind. I guess it has something to do with what Mr. Adams said on a videotape we saw recently, "We don't want our customers only to be satisfied, we want them to be delighted."

The company has been good to me too. I've had a lot of personal problems involving divorce and some other things. I was getting to the point where I believed that no one really cared. Then someone got me involved in a company-sponsored program that could arrange to have a psychologist talk to me. Since I didn't have a car, he came to see me at work after five o'clock, and we had a series of sessions until I was feeling better. It really impressed me just how much the company cared.

Little things seem to count too. When I was having problems with the height of my keyboard, somebody came in and changed it. And when I was bothered by the noise of the telephone operators, they moved me to a quiet position in front of a window. It's not that I am getting special favors or don't have to work hard. It's that they treat us as people.

This practice of setting good examples is promoted within Armstrong in at least two ways. One is by example. The skill and deliberateness with which senior managers serve as role models clearly signals to young managers the priority given this consideration. Another is coaching. This is typically done in the course of normal business dealings. For example, in supervising the plans and decisions of their subordinates, senior managers might openly consider the possible impact of the recommended actions on the organization's ethical climate so that everyone concerned can learn from the experience.

Access

Along with the various assertive methods employed to clarify and promote ethical standards—the pep talks, inspirational stories, and role models—Armstrong senior managers recognize the value in also being responsive to employees who might still be concerned or confused about ethical issues. The importance Adams assigns to employees having access to top people is evident throughout the organization. Managers at all levels encourage subordinates to speak out on questions of fairness and integrity. The following remark by a young female clerk is representative in describing the resulting effect: "When you run across an ethical problem, you can talk it over with your supervisor. You can also go to so many other people in the company to straighten things out. This really helps."

Allen Deaver, executive vice president, summed up his high regard for Armstrong's positive emphasis on ethical behavior in saying, "This company has values that you can almost see and taste. We care about people. You can always talk to someone at the top when something at work bothers you or interests you. You are not boxed in."

Discouraging Misconduct

Armstrong's attention to inspiring ethical behavior is matched by a diligent companion effort to discourage unethical behavior. One way senior management accomplishes this is through its efforts to avoid giving potentially misleading signals as to what is acceptable behavior. Equally important are its efforts to uncover and punish any violations of ethical standards.

Avoiding Wrong Signals About Ethical Behavior

Projecting a clear and unambiguous message about ethical behavior is a factor in management's thinking. Eugene Moore, manager of corporate information, made this point with the following illustration:

> It used to be okay in Florida to make political contributions, but illegal in other states. The plant manager in Florida wanted to make such payments because other firms in the area were doing so. The company decided to deny his request, even though legal and ethical, primarily because an exception to our general ban on political contributions could weaken this policy in the minds of our people elsewhere.

The problem of questionable appearances comes up in various ways and is not always so simple to avoid. A case in point was the concern of a senior executive about the possibility of giving the wrong impression on those occasions when it was necessary to spend time with the senior people of major suppliers in settings that had the appearance of a boondoggle. Whenever possible, he took along lower-level employees to the hunting lodge or golf resort so that the business-related content of the trip could be verified to his people."

Checking Performance and Punishing Violators

Armstrong maintains a control system that enables managers to check on performance in many ways. A quality assurance program has given visibility to additional dimensions of performance. In the course of their work, internal auditors are alert to ethical issues. These and other means are employed at all levels in the organization to detect mistaken and deliberate violations of ethical standards.

The company takes pains to make clear that violations will he punished. Strict enforcement is the rule for reasons revealed in the following accounts. A senior operating manager fired three shipping loaders when he learned that they had accepted a bribe to change the priority in loading trucks. His concern for the mens' families was outweighed by that of maintaining discipline and setting an example. A similar dilemma was handled by a marketing executive in much the same way when he learned that one of his senior salesmen had been submitting false expense reports. He explained, "Here was a man who had not told the truth and had been stealing. On the other hand, the amount of money was not large, the person had served the company well for 28 years, and I knew his family. For me, the deciding factor was to behave fairly with respect to the 23,000 other company employees who were playing by the rules."

Adams acknowledges that the most difficult discipline issues for him occur when people behave improperly to benefit the company with no direct personal gain involved. But even in those instances, people are punished to remove any question that might arise concerning the seriousness of Armstrong's ethical standards and avoid any possible misperceptions of special favors being given. While it might seem callous for a company to punish a person whose actions are not deliberately self-serving, for Adams it is even more wrong to jeopardize people's trust and confidence in senior management's firm commitment to high ethical standards.

The overall business ethics process at Armstrong World Industries is characterized by senior management's personal involvement in defining and encouraging ethical behavior on the one hand and detecting and punishing ethical misconduct on the other. This direct approach works particularly well in the Lancaster area, where senior managers are constantly engaged in reinforcing ethical standards, and where Amish and other rural communities have strong moral and work ethic traditions. The business ethics process appeared less robust in some operating units that were distant from headquarters. This observation underscores a need for senior managers to project and even replicate their ethical leadership in business units that fall outside their direct reach. One firm that succeeds in doing this well is Hewlett-Packard.

Hewlett-Packard

Hewlett-Packard, renowned for the style and effectiveness of its management, provides us with a somewhat different perspective in our examination of how ethical standards are reinforced and perpetuated in a company. While the lists of relevant activities found at HP and Armstrong would be very similar in content, they would differ markedly with respect to the relative emphasis senior managers assign to individual elements. In contrast to the somewhat directive approach at Armstrong, HP, with its need to manage highly skilled professionals in a rapidly changing business environment, attempts to create an organizational climate that can be spontaneous and self-directing in its support of the firm's ethical standards. For this purpose, emphasis is placed on creating a strong sense of belonging, encouraging initiative, and stimulating people's attention to the company's basic values. In this case, we examine two operating divisions located about 1,000 miles from the source of ethical leadership at headquarters.

Fostering Collegiality

It does not take long for a visitor to sense that people feel good about working for the Colorado Telecommunications Division of Hewlett-Packard. As a 23-year veteran of the company with responsibility for facilities maintenance put it, "If I didn't have to work, I wouldn't be here. But since I do have to work, then this is the best place to be. The people here are great. You can respect them and they respect you. This is true no matter what position a person holds in the company."

At HP, the notion of mutual respect comes up time and again and in various ways. For a traffic administrator, it has to do with having a voice in company affairs, "A person is not just another number here but is valued as an individual who can contribute. There is a recognition that ordinary people, not just managers, get things done. We feel that we participate in making many important decisions." For a secretary, it involves the absence of special trappings and perks for a favored elite, "Status was a big issue in other companies where I worked. On the executive floor, people got mahogany desks, brass nameplates, thick carpets, and were called 'Mister.' Here the division manager sits in an open office in the middle of the plant floor, and everyone is on a first-name basis."

This atmosphere is rooted in HP's managerial style. The company's strategy to compete on the basis of new technical contributions and the founders' preferences both favor a tradition of teamwork. With reference to the importance of teamwork at HP, David Packard said, "The only way this company is going to run successfully is if we can ensure that there is the maximum flow of information and cooperation between all the elements of it."[4]

To engender this vital cooperation and flow of information, HP senior management actively fosters an open and egalitarian work atmosphere. The use of first names and the elimination of perks are just some of the many ways this is done. Employees also mention picnics, the occasional surprise beer bust for celebrating good performance, and the company's wilderness recreation areas—where they can vacation in cabins built by fellow employees with materials supplied free—as ways HP encourages them to get to know each other better.

One notable custom that encourages employee interaction is the morning offering of free doughnuts and fresh fruit. Sue Skiffington-Blumberg, marketing communications manager, described the practice and what it means to her, "When HP was still a fledgling operation, the founders' wives used to bring cookies and doughnuts every day to the people in the shop. This thoughtful act in time became a custom, and HP would supply doughnuts and fruit every morning throughout the organization. Several years ago, during tight times, the company curtailed the practice to Wednesdays only, probably more to show the need for cost consciousness than to save money. The cutback was a major issue for many of the employees. This week, the company reinstated the daily offering of free doughnuts and fruit, and morale has gone up totally out of proportion to the monetary value of the benefit. I think the reason for this favorable impact is the symbolic value of the doughnuts and fruit. They seem to give the message, 'We still care about you.'"

This emphasis on collegial relationships and teamwork can contribute to ethical climate in several ways. First, the added responsibilities that a team approach offers people also gives them a heightened sense of belonging and control. By being treated in this inclusive and respectful manner, most people are encouraged to treat others accordingly. Second, the close bonding an individual develops with fellow employees can add powerful motivation to behave in ways that are likely to be admired and to avoid those that might cause shame. Third, working teams provide a favorable setting for combatting the problem of moral muteness discussed in Chapter 2. Where close and comfortable relations develop, people are more inclined to raise delicate ethical issues and consider how to deal with them. And fourth, the task orientation of most organizational teams enables their members to get beyond abstract expressions of moral ideals and decide on what constitutes ethically appropriate behavior in specific, concrete situations. For full effect, however, employees must be clear about the values and standards that are to motivate behavior. Senior HP operating executives attempt to clarify and reinforce corporate values in a variety of ways.

Training Programs and Self-Examination

Hewlett-Packard's ethical values are defined and promoted in various corporate training programs. For example, all new employees attend a day-long program called "Working at HP" in which they are introduced to the organization's values as well as to its policies and practices. In recent years, HP has sponsored a series of management seminars culminating in one that deals with leadership and values based on interviews of outstanding managers from all parts of the corporation. Highlighting a connection between corporate values and successful careers in HP undoubtedly helps raise the relevance and importance of the program in the eyes of aspiring managers.

The kind of impact such lessons can have on practice is well illustrated by the way Alan B. Steiner, general manager of the Colorado Telecommunications Division, coupled the leadership program with a special effort to rejuvenate and redirect his unit. He explained:

> We are currently trying to develop a mission statement and a vision of what we would like the division to be. This vision encompasses the division's place in its industry, the internal environment we would like, both physical and emotional, how ideal employees would feel and behave, and how ideal supervisors and managers would feel and behave. If we talk enough about vision, it will eventually become compelling to the organization. Understanding our values is necessary to make our vision operational.
>
> The task we have is to make our values operational. When we indicate mutual trust, what does it mean? How will I behave? How will you behave? What will be different in the way we behave? It is

this kind of thinking that we have to go through if we really are to operationalize these values.

Senior managers were first asked to identify the key divisional values. Lower levels of management were sequentially involved in recasting these values for their own needs. The reason for this procedure was to gain commitment throughout the organization. The people at lower levels were aware of this effort and generally quite positive in their reaction. One young staff member mentioned seeing her boss's list of values as well as her boss's boss's list and right up to division general manager. She remembered that "honesty" and "trust in each other" were high on each list. When asked if these discussions of values came across to her as meaningful or rhetorical, she unequivocally judged them real and sincere.

The values Steiner and his divisional managers were listing and examining reflected the values that had infused every aspect of HP's strategy, style, and performance since William R. Hewlett and David Packard founded the company in 1939 making electronic instruments in a garage. These values and their expression in company affairs are known as the *HP Way*. Hewlett, some years ago, described the HP Way in the following words.

> I feel that in general terms it is the policies and actions that flow from the belief that men and women want to do a good job, a creative job, and that if they are provided with the proper environment they will do so. It is the tradition of treating every individual with consideration and respect and recognizing personal achievements. . . . The dignity and worth of the individual is a very important part, then, of the HP Way.

Respect for employees and a celebrated participative management style that supports individual freedom and initiative while emphasizing commonness of purpose and teamwork are not only hallmarks of HP's operating style, they are also central to the company's ethical fabric.

Top Down Interventions

While the impetus for shaping HP's ethical behavior is largely dispersed throughout the organization as a result of the emphasis given to participation, senior management continues to exert a significant force in this regard through its various interventions in operations. In some cases its actions are directly concerned with upholding core values. For example, the formal Statement of Corporate Objectives makes clear the importance HP attaches to customer satisfaction.

> Our fundamental goal is to build positive, long-term relationships with our customers, relationships characterized by mutual respect, by courtesy and integrity, by a helpful, effective response to customer needs and concerns, and by a strong commitment to providing products and services of the highest quality.

Colorado Telecommunications Division employees were all aware and supportive of this goal. Still, responsiveness to customers' needs and concerns was uneven until senior divisional line managers instituted the Sunrise Meeting. Under the resulting procedure, some two dozen manufacturing and technical managers and staff meet every Monday morning at 8:00 A.M. to review customer complaints that were received the preceding week. Specific responsibility for resolving each problem is assigned to one of the participants. By this simple but forceful intervention, senior management not only adds an effective mechanism for dealing with customer problems, it also reinforces in everyone's mind the importance of respect, courtesy, and integrity as core values.

Even when top down interventions are made for operational reasons, ethical issues are likely to arise and receive attention at HP. Efforts to change vendor relationships provide a good example. As is true for many U.S. industrial concerns, the Colorado Telecommunications (CTD) and Colorado Springs (CSD) divisions have both abandoned the practice of shopping multiple sources and instead have a close relationship with one or two vendors for particular items. The growing pressure for higher quality and lower costs spurred the various steps taken to improve the ability of selected vendors to supply HP's particular needs.

In 1988, both divisional managements examined the criteria for selecting vendors and the nature of the resulting new relationship. Andy Ouderkirk, CTD manufacturing manager, stressed the need to evaluate the strategic alignment and fit between a vendor's potential capabilities and commitments and HP's future needs. Hector Arrambulo, CSD materials manager, described the approach his department had developed to make this vital assessment of strategic fit, "Each vendor is now evaluated with respect to technology, quality, responsiveness, delivery, and cost. We also try to assess the quality of management and the economic strength of the enterprise."

This evaluation anticipates the increased intimacy between parties, "the getting in bed with the vendors" as one buyer characterized it. For example, HP buyers and materials engineers are spending more time at vendors' plants to assess performance and help improve their manufacturing operations. Vendor review sessions also take on increased importance as senior people from HP and its supplier firm jointly assess performance and plan for future requirements in detail.

Various ethical concerns were voiced at HP in connection with the increased exposure and dependence vendors would experience in the new relationship. As one buyer noted, "We shall have to be more careful than ever not to pass information from one vendor to another and not to create unrealistic expectations in terms of future purchases. When there are schedule changes, we are going to have to help them adjust. We can't just jerk these people around because they depend on us." These concerns for fair dealings also take HP's interests into account. Several buyers mentioned the increased difficulty they face in determining a true market price and the problem of getting vendors to pass on a fair portion of the savings that result from improvements in manufacturing and scheduling.

Clearly, problems still remain as the two divisions work out their new relationships with vendors. What distinguishes HP's efforts from those of many other companies is the ethical sensitivity that is shown in addressing these issues. This sensitivity, reflecting HP's fundamental values, is captured in the following comment by one of the buyers, "Looking out for the vendor's interest is part of my job, just as is looking out for HP's interest. 'Fairness' is the key word in this relationship."

Unintended Undesirable Consequences

Actions taken in support of ethical standards can sometimes lead to unintended, undesirable consequences. Hewlett-Packard encountered a dilemma of this nature in an attempt to enhance employment security. For many HP employees, the company's concern for employment security provides the strongest evidence of management's respect for them. As in the case of Lincoln Electric, employment security is a cornerstone of the firm's formal policy structure. However, in a business as dynamic as electronics, where volatility is unavoidable, achieving this goal requires considerable management care and effort.

When staffing has to be reduced, HP makes a special effort to minimize the ill effects on employees. For example, when the decision was recently made to close the PC board shop in the Colorado Springs Division, the 100 employees affected were offered opportunities either to move to the company's other PC board shops at Loveland, Colorado (about 150 miles from Colorado Springs), Boise, Idaho, and California, or to find other employment in the division. The transition was scheduled to occur over a year's time. A personnel manager described a more serious reduction of workforce that the division had made several years earlier. "When the need to restructure and to downsize the division was finally acknowledged, management worked hard to treat the employees with care and compassion. Incentives were given for voluntary separation, and people were reassigned where possible. For those persons ending up in lower-paying jobs, wages were reduced gradually over a transition period. Our workforce went from 2,700 to 2,200, but nobody was told to leave HP against his or her will." A manager of purchasing who had worked for several other large industrial firms observed in this connection "that HP tends to agonize over relocation problems."

As changes in technology and competition accelerated, senior management increased the use of temporary help to avoid some of the staffing disturbances that mounting workload fluctuations would cause. While HP's concern for employment security was a matter of pride throughout the company, this hiring practice made some employees uncomfortable. One middle-level technical manager raised an issue of fairness. "The temporary employees were recently excluded from company parties because of potential legal problems. Apparently, if they are included in all our social functions, their temporary status could be challenged in court. I can understand that, but it runs counter to our general attitude of fairness and equity in the company. How can I work side-by-side with people for months on end and then tell them that they are not welcome to join in the celebrations? It's not right." Clearly, some of HP's most cherished values come into conflict in this practice.

As viewed by the technical manager, ensuring job security for regular employees is commendable, but creating a second-class order of temporary employees to achieve this end is not. Senior managers need to be on the lookout for such unintended negative consequences. Failure to deal with inconsistencies and contradictions of this nature can be costly in terms of damage to people's confidence in management's integrity.[5]

Exploiting Other Corporate Activities

While senior managers in the firms studied were generally comprehensive in their efforts to reinforce ethical standards, in a number of instances they overlooked important opportunities. Almost everything that goes on in an organization can influence its ethical climate in one way or another. As noted in Chapter 2 in connection with ethical sensitivity, certain activities, such as corporate quality programs, are particularly rich in their manifest and potential connections to ethical behavior. For example, senior management's resolve to provide quality products and services has fairly obvious ethical implications in the firm's relationship with its customers. Total quality management programs can also affect how employees are treated and how they treat each other. This important consequence is evident in the following remark by an order services supervisor.

> In the last few years I find that the atmosphere has been more open, and I think it is a result of the quality program. There has been an emphasis on managers communicating with the people who actually do the work. We used to feel that our opinions were considered worthless. That is no longer true. The result is we have a greater sense of comfort and security in our jobs.

A young research manager noted how employees treated each other more positively as a result of senior management's attention to quality.

> The quality program also affected our thinking by having people work together in new ways. Years ago, we operated like a caste system, with professionals and nonprofessionals not mixing. Now we put together teams involving all kinds of people to deal with specific problems. As a result of working together, we now see each other more as equals, and we're more sympathetic to the other person's problems.

Each of these companies could have used its quality program to much greater effect in reinforcing ethical behavior had management been more explicitly aware of the potential connections between the two processes. Some idea of the possibilities was evident at Corning, where a quality program initiated in 1983 became widely recognized as a "culture change phenomenon." According to David Luther, senior vice president and director of quality, "Concern with quality in our minds does not only apply to the factory floor but as well to behavior throughout the company. It concerns every aspect of how we work with each other on a day-to-day basis and over time." One example of how Corning puts into effect this concern with working relationships is a practice motivated by the quality program, whereby higher-level managers regularly communicate with people at the lowest levels of the organization to detect "potential problems, strained relationships, and the need for more effective leadership." Activities of this nature can provide valuable reinforcement to an ethics program.

The problem is that much of this potential is frequently overlooked by those engaged in developing organizational commitment to business ethics. Few companies fully exploit the obvious connections between quality programs and business ethics. Not surprisingly, less obvious opportunities tend to be totally missed. A recent decision at Texas Instruments (TI) to change from a monthly closing of the budget to a quarterly basis provides a good example of a major organizational undertaking where the favorable ethical consequences were unintended and even unrecognized when they occurred.

The TI budget was highly detailed with its 200 to 750 line items. The budget review normally comprised three distinct elements: (1) the comparison of actual results with forecasted figures; (2) an analysis of the variances; and (3) a reforecasting of the budget. Marvin Lane, vice president and corporate controller, explained the principal reason for the change in practice as of 1988, "Too much management time and effort were being devoted to measuring monthly performance. We decided to follow in the footsteps of Dow Chemical and General Electric in changing to a quarterly detailed review." The resulting freed-up time was widely acknowledged as beneficial to operational productivity.

The change in the budget review procedure seemed also to have at least two favorable consequences with respect to ethics. By removing the need to meet prescribed sales and delivery targets each and every month, management removed some of the pressures that could motivate unethical action on the part of sales and manufacturing people. A manufacturing manager who had worked at TI for more than 20 years explained these pressures and their consequences in a semiconductor manufacturing operation.

With a month-to-month need to meet forecasts, pressure was always stepped up near the end of the month. This meant driving the people harder and going into overtime. To some extent there might have been some slippages in the quality of the product shipped out, but these were only marginal, never serious.

The real problem, to my mind, was the message we were giving our workers. When we stepped up the pressure to get the stuff out the door, they would perceive management as not really quality conscious. At the end of the month you could always hear someone muttering, "How come all month we talk quality and at the end of the month all we ever hear is to get things out the door?" This apparent contradiction no doubt caused workers to lose confidence in how truthful their supervisors and managers were. The fact that quality was not ever really seriously compromised was lost in the turmoil of pushing the goods out.

This perceptive assessment shows how the monthly drive to meet targets can undermine the climate of trust so important to ethical conduct. The fact that quality standards are upheld is a credit to the managers and supervisors in this department, but the recurrent need to make close calls on quality puts a severe strain on these people. This strain was seen as an ethical issue by at least one concerned manager. "I'm bothered about putting the department in a pressure cooker the end of every month. How does it affect the people? Even the overtime bothers me since it keeps these men and women from their families." Under the new budget review schedule, these pressures are still likely to arise each quarter. However, the extension of the normal work period between "pressure cooking" from approximately 25 days with the monthly review to 80 or 85 days with the quarterly review not only reduces significantly the number of times that organizational unity and trust is placed under strain, but also gives the organization more than triple the recovery time.

The second favorable consequence of the budget review change on TI's ethical climate has to do with the relationship between the middle and upper levels of management. In relaxing the oversight process, senior managers are showing greater confidence and trust in their subordinates. Some of the benefit that flows from this expression of respect is revealed in the following remark by a divisional general manager: "In a funny way, if anything, I feel even more compelled to meet targets than before. I don't want to let down my boss after he gave me this extra freedom to act. I think that our appreciation of the benefits of this change will take place over time without notice. The only way that they would become readily apparent would be if management were to reverse from quarterly to monthly review. People would then feel the loss of trust." The increase in trust nourishes mutual respect and has a positive effect on ethical as well as business behavior.

The change in budget review schedule also has certain drawbacks. A senior line executive who favored the change noted, "We used to spend much too much time reviewing budgets, and now we have some time freed up for other work. On the negative side, we have lost some of our rapid response to problems. We have also lost the monthly linearity of our output." Some division and department managers continue to review their units on a monthly basis. One of them valued the monthly review as an opportunity for his managers to help one another in uncovering and solving problems.

In this case, the net effect of the budget process change on ethical behavior appears quite positive, even without senior management's actual awareness of the connections. In other cases, the balance might not be favorable without deliberate efforts to make it so. Broadly considered, much of the potential benefit that could be gained in managing a major organizational effort so as to reinforce a firm's ethical position is likely to be lost if senior managers are not sensitive to the possibilities and consequently fail to exploit the opportunity.

Community Service: General Mills

The policies and practices by which the companies in this study reinforce ethical behavior are similar in content, if not always in emphasis. There are, however, some exceptional activities, such as those associated with General Mills' active involvement in community service.

While many people would applaud the company's achievements in community service, others would question the commitment of corporate resources for that purpose. There are some who would even question the connection between community service and corporate ethics. The retort of H.B. Atwater, Jr., chairman and chief executive officer of General Mills, to this objection is that he and his executive group view the communities in which the company operates and society at large as one of the four constituencies that it must serve—along with customers, employees, and shareholders—to be successful in the long run. He holds that corporate citizenship involves self-interest as well as a moral imperative.

Corporations are, under law, U.S. citizens and enjoy thereby both the duties and privileges of citizenship. If we believe that no one of us can prosper in an unhealthy society, it follows that every citizen, individual or corporation, should contribute toward the betterment of society. In the long run, this is a proposition of self-interest and is thoroughly consistent with our duty to shareholders.[6]

The community setting in which Atwater and most of the firm's senior officers work helps to explain the company's emphasis on this aspect of ethical concern.

The maintenance of the Company headquarters in the Minneapolis-St. Paul business community has kept General Mills in an environment that has consistently encouraged responsibility to society, support of the arts, education, and social services, and enlightened attitudes toward competitive practices and employee relations. Aggressive activities by executives heading the area's leading companies have resulted in companies competing with each other in support of community activities. The senior officers of many of the area's leading companies work together on the boards of non-profit organizations and encourage, if not cajole, each other to high levels of community involvement.[7]

The two primary forms of community involvement for General Mills are corporate philanthropy (or grant making) and employee volunteerism. With respect to gifts and grants, the company, acting directly or through a professionally staffed corporate foundation, concentrates foremost on education and social welfare and to a less extent on the arts. (In 1992, General Mills devoted the equivalent of 3 percent of domestic pre-tax income, almost $16 million, to charitable activities.)

Employee volunteerism is not only encouraged in General Mills, it is virtually required. Atwater's explanation of why and how this came about—drawn from his remarks in accepting for General Mills the Harvard University sponsored George S. Dively Award for leadership in corporate public initiative—furnishes an instructive model for how senior managers can increase an organization's sensitivity and commitment to a particular area of ethical consideration.

At General Mills we believe that nothing worthwhile can be accomplished without personal commitment. . . . To be effective, commitment must be shared throughout the company. . . .

To involve our Board of Directors in corporate citizenship and to demonstrate their commitment we have a Public Responsibility

Committee of the Board, made up of outside directors. Management reports to this committee on a regular basis concerning its corporate citizenship policies and programs.

An essential element to achieving corporate citizenship objectives is integration within and throughout the entire company. This may sound obvious, but traditionally much of American industry has found it convenient to delegate these matters to the Public Relations or Community Affairs departments. The implication was unmistakable: "Turn it over to staff and let's get on with the job of running the company."

Very frankly, this was the way General Mills operated for many years—most of our key managers were not involved in the company's social outreach—having no responsibility, they likewise had limited interest.

In our efforts to change this mind set, we began with a revision of the set of objectives which each executive submits at the start of the fiscal year. These objectives are the bench mark to measure accomplishment for cash incentive purposes. We had historically asked for specific objectives in three broad areas:
- Current financial performance
- Long-term strategy
- Manpower development

We now include a fourth section headed "External Involvement." Each executive must now list objectives for personal civic and community activity—he or she knows that we regard this as an important part of the job.[8]

In tying community work to performance evaluation and compensation, management aligns personal self-interest with community citizenship in a powerful way. To facilitate employee involvement in educational, health-care, family support, and other areas of community need, a unit of the Public Affairs Department collects and matches known needs of not-for-profit organizations with the interests and talents of General Mills people.

General Mills combines grant making and employee involvement through its pioneer concept of charitable investments. The idea is to fund programs where, with active management, the company can recoup the investment over time, thereby enabling it to commit monies exceeding its grant-making capacity. Atwater described this concept with reference to the initial program.

. . . To guide and preserve our investment we expect substantial involvement of line managers. In a sense our contribution is the foregone interest on our investment and the time of our managers, coupled with the substantial investment risk that we may not get our capital back.

We came upon this idea in the early 1970s when a local consortium of business leaders turned down a loan for the rehabilitation of a large residential area near downtown Minneapolis. We decided to go it alone, not only because the neighborhood was the key to the stability of downtown, but also because we were convinced that we could do the same job by using the same talents and disciplines that served us well in the profit sector.

Over a period of several years we invested some $8 million in the Stevens Court neighborhood. This amount is probably 100 times more than a typical grant could have been. We ended up owning some 26 apartment buildings and over 700 individual units. Along the way we encountered opposition and hostility from organized labor, city hall, minority groups, and some residents of the neighborhood itself.

After being involved for a decade, we sold Stevens Court to private owners, but not before the neighborhood was stabilized. We essentially broke even and considered then—and now—that the project was a success. We made a difference in solving a problem that under no circumstances could have been met through conventional philanthropy.[9]

The Stevens Court experience motivated management to seek another self-liquidating program that could benefit the community. Three task forces spent over one year evaluating more than 65 individual projects, including housing, health and related care for the elderly, and computer-based education for high-school dropouts. Long-term care for the elderly was finally chosen, and General Mills, in collaboration with a leading health care operating foundation, set out to explore alternatives to the traditional nursing home. The General Mills annual report for 1986 gave the following account of this effort.

The nation's elderly are the focus of Altcare, a joint venture begun in 1983 with the Wilder Foundation of St. Paul, Minn. Altcare has been the catalyst for Elder Homestead, a 28–unit alternative to the nursing home, opening in a Minneapolis suburb this fall. If the prototype proves successful, it will be replicated elsewhere. Altcare has also played an important role in the success of the nation's first senior HMO [health maintenance organization] specializing in long-term care, and is planning an Alzheimer's Care Network.

Early in 1988, Altcare was honored by President Reagan as one of the winners of the President's Citation Program for Private Sector Initiatives, the highest honor in the nation for community outreach programs.[10]

In parallel with these efforts to be more creative in community involvement were other efforts to include more communities. Dave Nasby, director of community projects, explained this second thrust, "General Mills has a long and impressive involvement in community affairs in the Minneapolis-St. Paul area because the top people are involved and committed. We have been much less active in other localities where we operate and are striving to change that. The company used to spend 90 percent to 95 percent of its grant money locally, now that amount is down to 60 percent or 70 percent. Recently, for example, the company identified a need for human services for Hispanics in South Chicago." To the extent that community service can reinforce the ethical standards of an organization, spreading these efforts to other geographical areas of operation helps to spread senior management's moral leadership throughout General Mills.

Atwater makes the case for a company engaging in community service on the grounds of its responsibility to society and even of self-interest in fulfilling its obligations. The case can also be argued with respect to the favorable impact such activities can have on a firm's ethical climate. One benefit of community service can be its uplifting effect on the attitude and morale of the people making the effort. Moreover, doing good deeds in the community can motivate people to think more about their own behavior in other settings and to be more sensitive to others. Andrews makes this connection in his report on ethics at General Mills. "That widespread involvement in community affairs is thought to be relevant to ethical business practice is illustrated by one executive's comment that he found it hard to imagine that a person who read to the blind at night would cheat on his expense account the next day."[11]

A second and possibly more important benefit is the favorable impact senior management's concerns for community service can have on organizational trust. Earlier the point was made about how ethically improper or questionable behavior by management in one regard could undermine people's trust and confidence in its integrity and commitment to ethics in general. Here we see an example of positive reinforcement, where management's genuine concern and respect for people in the community can help employees to believe in its sincerity concerning other ethical issues.

Some Lessons from Practice

Several general observations can be made from the recounted experiences of how senior managers at Armstrong, Hewlett-Packard, and General Mills reinforce ethical standards. One is the significant time and attention they devote to these efforts. As a rule, these managers engage frequently in a wide variety of activities to demonstrate their commitment to business ethics and to instruct and inspire others to a similar commitment. With reference to Bill Adams' simile, it takes a lot of little pushes to keep the ethical flywheel from slowing down. However much time and attention senior managers devote, ethical problems can still arise unexpectedly and ethical violations are bound to occur. What this points to is the importance of constant vigilance and timely intervention on the part of managers and business leaders who are skillful in fostering the firm's ethical standards.

A second consideration has to do with organizational fit. As revealed in the comparison between Armstrong and HP, where and how the flywheel gets pushed makes a difference. The relatively stable competitive environment, the high proportion of non-exempt employees, and the large concentration of operations near headquarters led Armstrong to be fairly directive in its approach. At HP, volatile business conditions, large numbers of highly educated professional employees, and the geographic dispersion of operations favored activities encouraging self-direction. As these experiences indicate, senior managers need to take into account the particular circumstances for their firm in deciding on an overall approach to reinforcing ethical standards and on where and how they can have the greatest impact on the organization.

A third observation concerns underexploited and unexploited opportunities to reinforce ethical standards. Major corporate programs designed to improve quality, productivity, and other critical dimensions of business performance typically have significant ethical implications. When such programs are pushed hard and done well, they also can strengthen an organization's ethical climate. In almost all the companies studied, senior managers missed important opportunities to exploit such potential reinforcement. What we can learn from this failure is the need for senior managers to consider how any specific program or activity that significantly affects organizational attitudes and behavior could be made to relate constructively to the firm's ethical standards.

The final observation concerns the ethical conflicts and dilemmas that can arise as managers engage in a variety of activities to reinforce ethical standards. These activities generally tend to reinforce each other. For example, the attention Armstrong's executives pay to setting good examples contributes to a rich lore of inspirational stories. These stories in turn are prominently featured in senior management's pep talks. But, as we have seen, ethical policies and actions also can be in conflict with each other, leading to unintended and undesirable consequences. The difficulties in using temporary employees at HP was cited as an example of this problem. Potential ethical conflicts are often not so apparent. For example, considering community service from the individual employee's perspective, is it ethical for General Mills, through the performance appraisal process, to forcibly involve an employee who is simply not interested in such activities? What about the person who is unable to participate because of family obligations, such as having to care for an invalid parent or spouse? Another example is Armstrong management's view that strict application of punishment for unethical behavior is necessary to demonstrate the company's resolve in these matters and as a point of fairness to all those who played by the rules. But what is just treatment of a culprit whose actions might have been induced by a perceived pressure from a superior or in the heat of a genuine overenthusiasm to reach a goal?

The presence of such dilemmas should not be seen as refuting the important role that policies and practices can play in motivating ethical behavior. Instead, such dilemmas often are a sign that the policies and practices are functioning well in touching on every aspect of corporate life, bringing to the surface the inevitable conflicts that must be resolved.

5

Involving the Right People

A vital element in the framework for managing corporate ethics is staffing an organization, especially positions of authority, with ethically minded people. In the companies studied, this factor was widely credited as being one of the principal reason for corporate ethical behavior. The reasoning was straightforward: business ethics ultimately depends on the moral inclinations of the people doing the work of the corporation; no ethics program, however good, can succeed if the people involved do not value the basic ethical precepts. Considering the importance senior managers appear to assign to the moral quality of their people, it is surprising just how little explicit attention is given to this matter, even in companies that are proud of their ethical people.

Building an organization of ethical people requires senior managers to act on three fronts. First, they must attract people with integrity to the firm and to select them for employment. Second, they should help employees to relate to their basic moral values to their business responsibilities. Third, they have to provide for future ethical leadership by identifying people who are effective in motivating others to behave ethically and placing them in positions of responsibility. This chapter examines each of these requirements and describes how some of the companies studied approach hiring, the development of personal values, and leader selection to further organizational commitment to business ethics.

Attracting and Selecting Ethical People

The starting point in staffing an organization with moral people is to attract and hire such people. To an extent, this process occurs naturally. Firms that are known for their upright dealings are likely to attract people with strong moral values. More than one employee interviewed said in effect, "One of the major things that attracted me to this company was that it was ethical." But ethical companies that are financially and commercially successful also attract individuals who are relatively unconcerned about ethics. These people need to be screened out in recruiting. The importance of this kind of selection was uppermost in the mind of W. Michael Blumenthal, chairman of Unisys, when he reflected on the mistakes and regrets of his 36–year career in business, government, and academia: "When did I make my greatest hiring mistakes? When I put intelligence and energy ahead of morality."[1]

Mistakes of this nature are costly in two regards. First, as Blumenthal implies, people lacking moral character can hurt the organization through improper actions or failures to act. He defines moral character as an ability to sense what is right and what is wrong, a willingness to be truthful, and courage to say what one thinks and do what is right. Although these remarks were made with reference to high-level executive positions, the importance of personal character applies throughout an organization. Employees at all levels have to be able to trust their colleagues—peers, subordinates, and superiors—to function effectively. The second detriment to hiring people of questionable character is the demoralizing effect it can have on other employees. The apparent disregard of standards signified by such hirings can undermine organizational confidence in senior management's ability, if not its sincerity, to provide ethical leadership.

If good practice calls for concerted efforts to attract and hire people with strong moral values and to repel and reject ethical weaklings, then a firm needs to assess the moral character of candidates for employment and to use this measure as a major criterion for selection. Common practice falls short on both counts, if the following evidence about the management recruiting practices in the companies studied is any indication of what happens in other companies. Each person who attributed his or her company's ethical performance to the quality of its people was asked at an unrelated point in the interview to describe recruiting practices and the criteria for selection. The following response by a sales manager was typical. "We want to know how well a person has done academically and about extra-curricular activities. We are looking for a person with enthusiasm, who is self-disciplined, who will work hard, and who wants to win." Almost everyone mentioned such personal qualities as intelligence, initiative, and drive. Almost no one mentioned moral character.

When the absence of moral character from the list of explicit criteria for hiring was pointed out, the persons being interviewed responded in one of three ways. About half of them took refuge in the belief that moral character was assessed implicitly during the course of the job interviews by how comfortable the recruiters felt with the applicant. A slightly smaller number were of the opinion that moral character could not be properly assessed in an interview, or even in the course of several interviews, and would have to be tested and calibrated over time on the job. Finally, a few were taken aback by the observation and admitted to an inconsistency between their pronouncements on the importance of employing ethical people and their company's recruiting practices.

Admittedly, it can be difficult if not impossible to get a clear reading on a person's moral character in an interview.[2] After all, the applicant normally is trying to make a favorable impression. Few people would admit outright to being unethical. Nonetheless, in the course of discussion, there often are subtle signs that can provide useful information about a person's values to interviewers who are sensitive to such matters and actively on the lookout. This is not to say that every clever scoundrel can be uncovered. But as the experience of Mark Twain Bancshares shows, a deliberate effort to recruit highly principled people does make a difference.

Mark Twain Bancshares

The moral character of Mark Twain's employees was of particular importance to senior managers for several reasons.[3] Carl Wattenberg, corporate counsel, noted one reason common to banking in general. "Because banks deal with money, the industry is ripe for con deals. Growing alcohol and drug problems lead to more frequent and more desperate attempts at embezzlement. While security measures are important, the only way a bank can really protect itself is by making sure it employs honest and intelligent people."

Mark Twain's physical layout and staffing practices added to its vulnerability regarding security. The geographical spread of banking facilities to serve neighborhood communities, credited as a major reason for Mark Twain's rapid growth and strong competitive position, physically removed operating officers from the direct influence and oversight of senior managers. While a variety of measures were employed to provide safeguards, the reduced interactions, which could only increase the opportunity for misdeeds, placed a greater burden on personal integrity.

Adding to the problem was Mark Twain's practice of promoting very young people to positions of significant responsibility. Many of its bank presidents were in their thirties, some having reached that level while still in their twenties. The short professional track record for such people could only provide limited information about the business and moral judgments they might make in difficult situations. For this reason, senior managers had to rely on other means for assessing and further developing these critical faculties. The efforts to build a cadre of managers with strong ethical principles began in recruiting.

Throughout the company's history, founder Adam Aronson had been exceptionally active in recruiting. He had personally interviewed every undergraduate and graduate student candidate for a managerial job for almost twenty years and continued as chairman to interview at key schools. John Dubinsky, chief executive officer, described the college recruiting effort, "What we are looking for are young men and women who are bright with high verbal skills, strongly motivated, attractive (with a sparkle in the eye), family and community-oriented, and ethical. Since we only recruit at the best schools, we can easily reassure ourselves as to their intelligence. What is difficult to measure is their motivation and their moral character. To deal with those dimensions, we have several people interview each candidate and then compare notes." In his view, the extra difficulty resulting from having to assess young people without track records was more than offset by the advantage in getting them before they had much opportunity to develop questionable work habits or to become cynical about business ethics.

A junior loan officer who had participated in recruiting at his alma mater elaborated on Mark Twain's approach to recruiting. The recruiting party at Northwestern University had comprised the chairman, the CEO, the senior loan officer, two regional managers, and four others. He explained how the members interacted, "Right after the interviews, we all met to discuss each candidate. Usually, four or five of the nine would have met with any one student." Each interviewer seemed to have his or her own way for assessing moral character. One would examine a candidate's extra-curricular interests to learn what motivated that person and what that person valued. Another focused on a person's interest and concern for his or her family. The particular approach for judging an individual's ethical bias was probably less important than the amount of attention given to this assessment.[4]

Management's efforts to evaluate moral character and to attract people with high ethical standards made a perceptible impact on the candidates. Frank Trotter, head of bond trading recalled his experience. "When I was interviewed in 1981, Bob Butler [executive vice president] spent over an hour plying me with questions. At the end, he explained that he had not been trying to find out what I know so much as what kind of person I was. That really impressed me." Another young bank officer mentioned how he had been struck during the interview by Dubinsky's [CEO] discussion of whether or not to lend money for the construction of an abortion clinic as an example of the bank's thinking on such sensitive issues. Brian Call, a junior loan officer who had previously served as a Morman missionary, also recalled the emphasis that had been placed on ethical values during the interviews, adding, "What struck me was the genuine interest Adam [Aronson, chairman] and the other senior people had in me and my family as people. I had just interviewed a major New York bank where I felt that my wife and child were viewed as a possible burden to my career. In contrast, Mark Twain saw my family as a plus. That said a lot to me about the people in Mark Twain and their values."

While this study failed to uncover any special interview techniques for evaluating the moral character of unknown candidates, it did show that recruiters who attempt to make this kind of assessment can do so to advantage.[5] The process admittedly requires difficult judgments subject to error. Nonetheless, it stands to reason that intelligent and experienced interviewers are likely to be more successful in selecting ethical people by considering the moral dimension explicitly rather than vaguely or not at all. Moreover, as Mark Twain's experience indicates, the attention to ethics in recruiting has a benefit in highlighting for a new employee the relevance of personal moral values to future work experience.

Ethical Third Parties

The idea of staffing an organization with moral people can sensibly be extended beyond direct employees to include the selection of influential third parties—legal and financial advisors, management consultants, lobbyists, advertising agents, suppliers, distributors, and even customers—who are likely to uphold and support rather than subvert the company's ethical climate. In avoiding dependencies on unscrupulous outsiders, senior management eliminates potential sources of influence that might tempt or pressure people in the organization to cut ethical corners.

While few managers would admit even to themselves to hiring unscrupulous advisors or suppliers, "getting results" or "low price" can easily dominate the selection of such parties, with little attention to just how the job gets done. A subcontractor is engaged because it delivers on time at a low price. The fact that it hires illegal immigrants or employs exploitative labor practices can be easily overlooked or disregarded. A law firm is engaged because it has a reputation for winning certain kinds of cases. The firm's professional ethics might receive scant notice.

Associating with unprincipled third parties can be costly for the same two reasons as hiring unprincipled employees. Such advisors, agents, or commercial partners can cause a company to engage in unethical actions. Voluntary association with such parties can also undermine people's confidence in senior management's integrity as questionable or improper actions come to light and appear to be condoned. This consequence was colorfully summed up by a middle-level executive of a large corporation who complained, "How can [the CEO] claim to be so concerned about ethical behavior when he uses a sleazeball like that to orchestrate our legal defense in product liability?"

Developing Ethical People

Selective hiring is only a first step in developing an organization of ethical people. To exploit the benefits of private moral values for organizational purposes, management needs to help its people understand how their personal ethical standards apply to their work and encourage this application as ongoing behavior. If this connection is not made, much of the potential beneficial impact that ethically inclined employees might have on corporate behavior can fail to materialize. Moreover, given the diversity, complexity, and changing composition of ethical issues in business, there is also likely to be a need to extend and refine employees' thinking and values to encompass the company's ethical concerns.

Companies encourage the moral development of their people

in a variety of ways, including clearly articulating guidelines and standards (discussed in Chapter 3), providing ethical indoctrination and training experiences, creating conditions to strengthen employees' self-confidence in acting ethically, and using rewards and punishments to reinforce ethical behavior.

Indoctrination and Training

At Mark Twain, initial emphasis on ethical values in recruiting is quickly reinforced in two ways. First, all newly hired exempt employees are required to attend a Policy Study Group each Wednesday morning for a broad indoctrination to the company and its values. One young officer vividly remembered the moral pep talks Aronson gave at these meetings. Dubinsky led a discussion about various ethical issues relevant to Mark Twain's operations as part of the series, and the corporate legal officer reviewed the bank's nineteen-page document on ethical standards and conflict-of-interest policy. As a result of these discussions, every young officer knew the firm's ethical guidelines, the thinking and determination of its ethical leaders and watchdogs, and stories about one or more persons who had been fired for violating the rules and management's trust. The time devoted to instruction, the involvement of senior executives, the interweaving of ethical and business considerations, the quality of the program (comprehensive coverage, opportunities for discussions), and the formation of a closely knit peer group all contribute to making this experience highly memorable to young bank officers.

Socialization and instruction at Mark Twain are also realized through a tradition of frequent social gatherings involving all bank officers and their spouses. For many, this second level of reinforcement is a particularly powerful means of connecting personal and business ethics. Spouses are involved, and the values of senior executives are shared with newcomers on a personal basis through stories and discussions in a congenial setting. The resulting friendships and sense of family tend to heighten an individual's feeling of responsibility and desire for approval. As mutual trust grows, so does the potential for peer pressure and shame to serve as powerful deterrents to moral lapses.

Mark Twain's approach to ethical indoctrination is highly suitable for dealing with a small number of young, morally inclined college graduates who are entering management ranks. The task of connecting personal and business ethics is different and far more complicated when dealing with a large number of lower-level employees with heterogeneous backgrounds. In such circumstances, it becomes difficult if not impossible for senior executives to rely solely on personal persuasion and on their responsiveness to each person's questions and opinions. Formal training programs are required for developing employees' understanding, competence, and commitment with respect to ethical behavior on the job.

Successful business ethics programs vary greatly in length, content, and manner of presentation. However, they do seem to share at least two common characteristics. First, participants are given ample opportunity to ask questions, challenge assertions, and generally to engage actively in the learning process. One of the most common and harmful failings in connection with corporate ethical training sessions is violating this rule. In dealing with such complex matters as, for example, the regulations, laws, and sanctions that govern the work on government contracts, lecturing a group of 50 to 100 people for an hour and then taking questions for 10 to 15 minutes is tantamount to one-way communication. This all-too-common training format simply does not allow people to deal adequately with all the confusions and apprehensions that they might have.

A second common characteristic of successful training experiences is having a strong focus on ethical issues that are clearly relevant to the audience. Voicing moral platitudes and generalizations in corporate training programs is not likely to be effective in motivating interest, let alone involvement, in the corporate ethics process. A one-and-a-half day workshop organized by a Texas Instruments business unit could serve as a model in the application of these principles. Along with lectures and open discussions, three hours were devoted to group presentations on how to deal with specific case situations involving ethical problems. (See Exhibit 5-1 for an example.) Six hundred exempt employees were scheduled to participate in this workshop, 24 at a time.

Training, of course, can take many forms. One of the more innovative approaches for helping managers develop their sensitivity to important ethical issues is found in Armstrong World Industries. There, young, promising manufacturing managers are assigned to the personnel department for two or so years. Joseph Rempke, manager of industrial relations, explained this practice.

> Over the past forty years, the company has moved young, rising
> managers into personnel to give them an exposure to the employees'

CASES ON INTEGRITY EXERCISE

Case Study C

Just prior to an early morning operations review, you overheard your manager specifically instruct one of your employees not to raise any doubts regarding the extremely aggressive milestones that were previoulsy published for a project your employee manages. During the review, the employee expertly stays away from any mention of the questionable milestones. However, at the close of the pitch the customer (another TI project team) specifically asks: "How do you feel about your ability to meet the project milestones that were published earlier?" After a lenthy pause your employee states: "I have serious concerns about our ability to meet any of the milestones recently published." Immediately following the meeting, your obviously angry manager states: "We need to speak about this problem that your employee has now created. I think we need a new project leader. meet me in my office."

What do you do?

Exhibit 5–1 An ethics training exercise

point of view. This is especially important for people in production because they deal with so many workers. In this assignment, they are removed from the pressures of dollar costs and confronted with the human costs. A manager has to have both viewpoints to work effectively with people.

It also works the other way. I started in personnel, was then transferred to production, and eventually returned to personnel.

The opportunity for senior management to increase the ethical sensitivity of subordinates through job rotation can apply generally, not only to linking production and personnel. It stands to reason that the breadth of a manager's sensitivity to ethical issues is likely to correspond to breadth of business exposure and experience. With greater understanding of the jobs that employees in other functions must do comes greater understanding of the constraints and limits they face, including those that are ethical. For example, sales people who are knowledgeable about the production process are in a better position to avoid demanding unecessarily difficult delivery dates than those who are not so informed. The ethical consequences have to do with the excessive pressures that such demands put on the production staff and workforce and any resulting improper actions taken to meet the unwarranted goals.

Ethical Empowerment

Ethical indoctrination and training, however well conducted, are severely limited in the benefit they provide if employees lack opportunities to become involved in the process by which corporate ethical issues are raised and resolved. What is required are conditions that enable employees throughout the firm to engage in active and open consideration of work-related ethical issues.

Lincoln Electric gives a clear example of what might be called *ethical empowerment.* Through the functioning of the Advisory Board, workers have some voice in how they should be treated by the corporation. The company's egalitarian atmosphere—a common cafeteria, an open-door policy, and a hands-on management style—provides many other opportunities for all employees in the course of the working day to engage in the company's ethical formation. They can raise questions and become better informed about ethical issues, voice objectives about positions with which they disagree, and express or affirm their support of positions they favor.

The importance of active and open discussions about ethical matters throughout the firm cannot be overstated. According to Bird and Waters, "It is impossible to foster greater moral responsibility by business people and organizations without also facilitating more open and direct conversations about these issues."[6] Facilitating more open and direct conversations about ethical issues, in some cases, can entail far more than merely providing permission and forums for involvement. Take, for example, low-level employees, who despite good intentions and sincere efforts, are unproductive or belittled in what they do. Such people, vulnerable and lacking in dignity, understandably face pressures for survival that can overwhelm any concerns that they might otherwise have for the rights and welfare of others. Before they can engage properly in a corporate ethics program, the company needs to help them gain the esteem and security that would make them valued members of the organization. This connection was evident at St. John's Hospital in Lowell, Massachusetts, where the housekeeping women became more caring of patients' needs as they themselves were helped to become more productive and valued in their jobs. In such cases, corporate ethics is affected in at least two important ways. One is in helping low-status, poorly treated workers gain self-confidence and dignity in their jobs. The other is in improving service and giving full value to the customers (hospital and patients in this instance).

At St. John's Hospital and in similar situations, senior management at ServiceMaster is able to improve the productivity, morale, and ethical concerns of a workforce that tends to fall short on all three counts under less sensitive and gifted supervision.[7] While the following discussion focuses primarily on low-level workers who are easily taken for granted, the principles involved here have much wider application, dealing as they do with upgrading an employee's dignity, competence, and self-confidence.

The ServiceMaster Company

The ServiceMaster Company contracts with hospitals, schools, and industrial firms to supervise their service workers—such as housekeeping, laundry and linen distribution, food service, plant operations and maintenance, materials management, and clinical equipment maintenance. In addition, it franchises individuals to provide a range of on-site carpet cleaning, lawn care, and pest control services to residential and commercial customers. In 1992, the company, employing 27,700 people and managing the work of over 100,000 service workers, had sales exceeding $3.5 billion and a record of profits that qualified it as one of the leading large firms in the United States with respect to percent return on average equity during the previous decade.

The company's ability to achieve higher quality performance at a lower cost is the principal reason for its rapid growth. Its appeal also rests on the positive effect it has on a client's work atmosphere. In assessing her experience with ServiceMaster, Sister Maria Loyola, president of St. John's Hospital, remarked, "What I like best about the company is that they make our people feel important. They do this in many ways. For example, they give awards for such things as cleanest cart and cleanest room in the hospital. When they recently decided to introduce a new uniform, they had the employees select the uniform color. They really know how to motivate people to perform well."

C. William Pollard, president and chief executive officer of ServiceMaster, explained the significance of making people feel important in their job.

> Remember, you can buy a man's time. You can buy a man's physical presence at a given place. You can even buy a measured number of skilled muscular motions for eight hours a day. But you cannot buy enthusiasm. You cannot buy initiative. You cannot buy loyalty. You cannot buy a devotion of the hearts and minds and souls.

The significance as well as difficulty of this goal is heightened when we examine the people he has in mind. The workers ServiceMaster takes supervisory responsibility for typically are in entry-level positions and often are unskilled, uneducated, and even illiterate. Many do not speak English. Frequently, equipment is marginal, instructions poor, and supervision cursory. Work output is low, absenteeism and turnover high. These people are ill positioned to concern themselves about corporate ethics or much of anything else beyond holding onto their jobs.

In this situation, the task of connecting personal and business ethics requires far more than the indoctrination and team building that occurs at Mark Twain. ServiceMaster first has to build the individual worker's self-esteem, by giving each worker skills and support to improve job performance, and by inducing those served to value the work done and show their appreciation to the persons who do it—for example, getting hospital administrators, doctors, nurses, and patients to attach importance to the work performed by the housecleaning women at St. John's Hospital. To achieve all this, ServiceMaster strives to provide the housekeeping workforce with improved procedures and equipment, training, strong supervisory support, and recognition for the resulting quality performance. These coordinated efforts reinforce each other in practice.

Equipment, Materials, and Work Procedures
Key to ServiceMaster's efforts to improve worker productivity and service quality is to devise efficient work procedures and redesign equipment and materials in support of these procedures. This integrated approach to upgrading service delivery was described as follows.

> . . . By 1985 [the company's research and development department] had grown to a staff of 18 headed by two Ph.D.s. Its major functions were to study jobs and develop new equipment and materials for them.
>
> For example, one study led to the conclusion that for mopping in bathrooms, the mop should be sanitized with a fresh change of disinfectant each time before it was used. A special dispenser was designed for that purpose. In another study, it was found that a certain design of treated dry mop could perform a duty which previously consisted of both wet mopping and dry mopping in hallways.
>
> Most of the containers for cleaning materials were both color- and fragrance-coded for customers' employees who could not read.[8]

The cost savings and improved service quality resulting from refined equipment and procedures obviously benefit ServiceMaster with respect to customer satisfaction, client retention, and new contracts. These results also have an important effect on employees' morale as they gain a sense of accomplishment and experience more positive feedback in the form of fewer complaints and more compliments.

Training

To benefit from improved methods and materials, ServiceMaster conducts extensive on-the-job training programs for its clients' workers. While technical information bulletins and videos are prepared and used for instructional purposes, the one-on-one "you watch me, I'll watch you" training sessions conducted on-site by supervisors are at the heart of the job skills training effort. For example, damp mopping a corridor is taught by providing illustrated instructions coupled with a demonstration and followed by the "quarter in the corner" challenge. This challenge is described as a one-on-one session in which a supervisor throws a quarter into one corner of a room and challenges a customer's employee to mop the floor in one continuous "S" stroke, moving the quarter out the door. Those who are successful are awarded their quarters. Many employees are thought to still have them as trophies.

The importance of this training was clearly singled out by the facilities manager of a large new client institution when asked what benefit ServiceMaster had provided. "Training! Previously, we had zero training. One time we had a fellow use floor wax to clean the windows because he couldn't read. ServiceMaster is good at training. Not only does the work improve, morale also improves. After all, a person doing a good job feels good." Since making workers feel good about themselves is important to ServiceMaster, on-the-job training for clients' personnel includes classes on personal development, addressing subjects such as communications, self-esteem, and health. Workers are also encouraged to attend educational programs where they can learn to speak, read, and write English and develop themselves in other ways.

Recognizing and Rewarding Performance

ServiceMaster's attention to details, the zeal of its site managers, the special equipment and materials, and the organized training all contribute to a worker's sense of importance. But this kind of morale boost would soon dissipate if not reinforced by his or her own organization—the hospital, school, or industrial firm. The problem in this regard is that many people tend to disparage or take for granted work they consider to be menial as well as the persons doing such work. As a reminder of the drudgery of the work and the insensitivity with which low-level service workers are treated, all managers and supervisors are required to spend time each year in their charges' shoes. With reference to his own experience as a member of a custodial crew, Chief Executive Officer William Pollard described the demeaning way in which he had been treated:

> It's not uncommon, for example, for the person who is doing the housekeeping function to never be identified by [even a] first name, to almost be part of the woodwork . . . I'd be working in a busy corridor and I'd hear people talking about me—"He looks like a nice man. I wonder why he's doing this kind of work." Like I wouldn't be hearing them.[9]

ServiceMaster actively seeks to dispel such demoralizing feedback in a variety of ways. For example, each ServiceMaster site manager on occasion invites a senior person in the client organization to speak at a departmental meeting on the importance of the work performed by the service employees. The following account by a former site manager reveals the positive impact this practice can have.

> Some years ago I invited the head of surgery to speak to the custodial crew. At the meeting, he described the work he did in the operating room. He ended by explaining how the patient's recovery depended as much on the cleanliness of the post-operative surroundings as on his surgical work. These comments were inspiring to my people.
>
> Some of the greatest benefits, however, were yet to come. First, whenever he encountered custodial people, he would smile and ask how things were going. This unprecedented attention from an important personage was certainly noticed by my people and probably noticed by others.
>
> Then, some months later, some young surgeon screamed obscenities at one of my people when told nicely not to walk across a floor area being cleaned. When the head surgeon learned about the incident, he admonished the offending doctor in front of his colleagues for his insensitivity to the custodians as people and to the importance of their work. When we learned about this from one of the other young doctors, you could just imagine the effect on my people.

ServiceMaster helps key managers in the client organizations to appreciate the work of the service support employees in another way. Although its purpose is to ensure customer satisfaction, organized inspections make the support work highly visible, and thereby subject to acknowledgment and praise. Jim Huse, executive vice president in charge of ServiceMaster East Company, described the practice:

> One of the keys to ServiceMaster's success is based on its efforts to convey clearly to the customer what service it has received. The customer's representative is called upon to make a weekly inspection of the grounds and to grade the quality on a simple form made up for that purpose. The form not only allows the customer to indicate whether this or that is good, fair, or poor, but also to make specific comments and recommendations. The customer is then asked to sign this document. In a monthly joint review of the work and the program, the customer and ServiceMaster evaluate what has been accomplished during the past month, the objectives for the coming month, and any other items relevant to the relationship. Minutes are taken of this meeting and copies mailed to the customer for the record.
>
> One important benefit of this kind of feedback is to identify the particular biases of a customer. One customer might have a fetish about shining floors, another about not finding dust on top of bureaus. Only by getting the specific feedback can we know how to please the customer. The inspection then enables us to make the customer aware of the benefits it receives. As a result, service support people get to be regarded as valuable contributors rather than as burdens to operations.

Recognition and rewards are also emphasized by ServiceMaster in the normal course of its operations. Sister Loyola was earlier quoted commenting on the awards given "for such things as cleanest cart and cleanest room in the hospital." Outstanding workers and their spouses are also honored at an annual company conference.

The highest expression of recognition and reward was ServiceMaster's stated goal to have 20 percent of all its new management trainees come from the lowest ranks of its employees. According to Pollard, 16 percent of the firm's management had come from this source and several senior executives had started their careers with ServiceMaster "hauling trash or laundry, doing project work, or refinishing floors." A database that tracked the progress of over 120,000 health care, school, and industrial employees was available to assist managers in identifying likely prospects for promotion to management ranks. For many employees, what counted most was management's attitude. According to Caroline Bennet, in charge of custodial work at Eastern Nazarine College, "In ServiceMaster, there is a tendency to be positive and to build you up as a person."

Rewarding Ethical Behavior

In management, as with human behavior in general, studies and experience show that people are motivated by rewarding that which is desired and punishing what is not. Good management practice for developing ethical employees should recognize their ethical accomplishments with ample rewards (praise, perks, and promotion) and deprecate their misdeeds with discipline. Common practice, however, tends to give scant attention to rewarding ethical accomplishments.

In business, ethical behavior is widely perceived as a constraint instead of an opportunity. Senior managers often dwell on rules and strictures in framing the organization's ethical context. Subordinate employees come to regard the ethical dimension as a way to get into trouble, not a way to get ahead. The following responses to questions about the role ethical behavior plays in performance evaluation, assignments, and promotions are generally representative.

> Business ethics serves more as a veto than a plus. A person is expected to be honest and ethical so that it is not a factor in evaluation except to decide on terminating the relationship.
>
> > Department head,
> > Mark Twain Bancshares

> Good ethics is more or less a given. There is no positive reinforcement with respect to ethical behavior. You are only punished if you are caught out of line. All the rewards go the other way [for economic performance].
>
> > Division manager,
> > General Mills

There is nothing wrong in top management's wanting to make sure that employees do not act in ways that compromise the company's interests. But an overbearing emphasis on the "thou shalt not" often turns employees off. This effect is evident in the comments of a middle-level executive in one of the most highly regarded firms among *Fortune*'s 100 largest industrial corporations who complained during a dinner conversation that his company's code of conduct had become so detailed and so mechanistically promoted that he no longer knew or cared what it contained. This was true even though he had to sign a paper each year attesting to his familiarity with its contents to satisfy the legal department. In this instance, the manager, who otherwise appeared responsible and loyal to his company, viewed the procedure as a dumb, bureaucratic hassle. This experience is not uncommon in major U.S. corporations. Other executives reported similar reactions, observing in some cases, "All management wants is to make sure that I don't screw the company." And even more negative is the view that senior management is principally concerned with "covering its collective *[backside]*."

One manager, when asked why feedback on ethical behavior in his company focused almost exclusively on punishment for infractions, answered with the following interesting analogy. "Breathing is one of the most vital body functions for staying alive, but we don't really pay it much heed except when it is troubled. Ethical behavior is like breathing, it is or should be automatic." Although the simile is perhaps somewhat farfetched, it does make a valid point. When people are disposed to be ethical, moral considerations become so imbedded in every decision and action that they become commonplace and largely indistinguishable. As with breathing, the failure of ethical behavior is far more noteworthy than its enactment. There is a certain irony in this. Corporate ethics—something that should engender positive feelings and be inspiring—instead becomes negative and threatening for many employees as a result of the way in which their behavior is evaluated in practice.

There are, of course, exceptions to this pervasive negative bias in acknowledging ethical behavior. Occasionally, individuals receive favorable recognition for notable ethical actions. Their achievements might even serve as inspirational stories, becoming part of corporate lore. An example of a more systematic effort to accentuate the positive would be the inclusion of community service as an explicit criterion for performance evaluation in General Mills (discussed in the previous chapter). Contributors can be praised and rewarded as well as laggards admonished. Somewhat along the same lines, the performance evaluation form for managers and supervisors in Texas Instruments incorporates many explicit references to ethical conduct. For example, the most favorable evaluation category for the performance factor, *Motivation/*

Direction, includes the phrase *"Insists on the highest standards of ethical behavior."* Similarly, the definition for the factor *Judgement and Decision-Making* emphasizes the words *"Makes decisions and takes actions based on the highest legal and ethical standards."* While the mere inclusion of these ethically related measures does not assure that evaluators will give such considerations much weight compared to economic measures of performance, such references do invite a more even-handed treatment of ethical conduct with respect to positive and negative feedback.

These examples of positive reinforcement, while steps in the right direction, fall far short in tapping the potential benefits that senior managers could derive from more systematic and comprehensive reward practices in support of ethical behavior. If the companies studied are representative of above-average practice, then rewarding ethical behavior is possibly one of the least exploited opportunities for moral leadership.

Providing for Future Ethical Leadership

The most visible and consequential reward for ethical behavior is promotion to positions of higher authority. Over time, a systematic effort to advance otherwise qualified people who excel in their abilities to motivate ethical behavior is one of the most effective ways to inspire others to develop similar capacities and provide for future ethical leadership. For all its obvious promise, few senior managers pursue this effort to its full potential. Blumenthal's reflections on this point give some insight into the nature of the problem.

> I was too often impressed by the high intelligence and the substantive knowledge of an individual and did not always pay enough attention to the question of how honest, how courageous, and how good a person the individual really was.
> First of all, you have to give yourself plenty of time to observe a person. Second, you try to test him, make sure that you ask yourself that question about common sense and morality more deliberately, rather than not focus on it. It's very difficult. Sometimes when I would evaluate a person I would say, 'Boy, this guy is smart. Boy, this guy knows his stuff. He knows his brief. And boy, he's energetic. He's good in that job. Let's promote him.'
> Obviously, if I knew he was a crook I wouldn't have promoted him. But I didn't really stop to say, 'Now, there is another requirement. What do I really know about him? Do I really know enough?

Do I really know that he can handle the pressures and temptations?'
I didn't even think about it. I was dazzled, occasionally, by these
other qualities.[10]

As this comment reveals, it is not that Blumenthal or most senior
managers are unmindful or uncaring about the moral character of
the people who might be under consideration for positions of responsibility in corporate affairs. Indeed, most value it greatly.
Rather, they fail to focus deliberately in assessing this quality and,
like Blumenthal, become dazzled by a person's energy, intelligence,
or business track record.

In his letter of February 14, 1992, to GE share owners, Jack
Welch describes the choices and the dilemma senior managers face
in considering ethical qualitites as well as business performance in
evaluating leaders.

> In our view, leaders, whether on the shop floor or at the tops of
> our businesses, can be characterized in at least four ways.
> The first is one who delivers on commitments—financial or oth-
> erwise—and shares the values of our company. His or her future is
> an easy call. Onward and upward.
> The second type of leader is one who does not meet commit-
> ments and does not share our values. Not as pleasant a call, but
> equally easy.
> The third is one who misses commitments but shares the val-
> ues. He or she usually gets a second chance, preferably in a differ-
> ent environment.
> Then there's the fourth type—the most difficult for many of us
> to deal with. That leader delivers on commitments, makes all the
> numbers, but doesn't share the values we must have. This is the
> individual who typically forces performance out of people rather
> than inspires it: the autocrat, the big shot, the tyrant. Too often all
> of us have looked the other way—tolerated these "Type 4" managers
> because "they always deliver"—at least in the short term.[11]

The ongoing challenge for Welch and senior managers in general is
to foster Type 1 and to eliminate Type 4 leadership.

In reference to the costs associated with a lack of moral character in high-level executives, Blumenthal expresses concern about
their inability to handle pressures and temptations. These are important considerations to be sure, but there are also important
second-order consequences. The presence of amoral—or worse, immoral—persons in positions of authority can cripple or even de-
stroy an otherwise well organized program to raise ethical standards. Few things breed as much cynicism. Questions are bound to

arise as to how such people are able to survive and prosper in a company supposedly committed to ethical business conduct.

On the positive side, placing people of good character in positions of authority can benefit organizational life by the moral tone they set as role models. Time and again, people at all levels would tell of how their thinking about business ethics was shaped by their boss, often their first. For example, Craig Hattabaugh, a district sales manager for Texas Instruments, remembered a dilemma he encountered as a new salesman. "I had just gotten a big order for D-RAMs, but when I went to get the contract finalized, the purchasing agent wanted to change the contract in an improper way. When I told my boss, he said '____ him.' His willingness to forego a six hundred thousand dollar contract in order not to deal with an unethical character was an unforgettable statement to me about the ethics of this company." Much along the same lines, Melinda Stearns, a territorial representative for Armstrong noted, "My first manager was very ethical. For him, everything was black and white. This made a big impression on me on how to conduct business."

It would be difficult to exaggerate the importance of such inputs to a company endeavoring to promote ethical conduct. The local concern and commitment to ethical issues are so much more visible and forceful to the employees in that unit than any pronouncements from on high. As one manager astutely observed, "I am the company to my subordinates." Each manager can enhance or degrade the ethical climate for those parts of an organization on which he or she has an impact.

Indeed, ethical leaders can be found at any level in an organization. Texas Instruments is one corporation that recognizes and openly encourages this grassroots source of leadership.

> . . . we must always remember that when it comes down to the ethics of an organization, leadership can come from any TIer at any level. Whatever your job, if you are in a position where you can impact the work activities of others, then you can influence their ethics, as well.[12]

Good practice calls for senior management to recognize ethical leadership wherever it might be found in the organization. As with any other valuable asset, corporate leaders have an obligation to develop and use such potential ethical energizers to their full capacities. Those people who are good at motivating ethical behavior in others should be identified, rewarded, and deployed to areas of relevant opportunity or need just as is done for managers with special commercial talents. Happily, promoting ethical leadership within management's ranks need not be in conflict with the obvious need to promote commercial leadership.

Qualities of an Ethical Leader in Business

What kind of people should those responsible for developing the ethical leadership of the firm be on the lookout for? Qualities of the ethical leaders in the organizations studied give some answers to that question. Almost to a person, they are excellent business practitioners. As discussed earlier, a well-run and well-positioned enterprise capable of achieving its goals by honorable means provides a favorable climate for managing corporate ethics. A second impact that strong business capabilities can have on a company's ethical performance involves trust. When people can respect the business competence of a firm's leaders, they are more likely to have confidence in the quality and continuity of their ethical leadership as well.

This confidence in the ability of senior managers to provide sound and secure ethical leadership depends on a number of morally related personal qualities as well as business competence. The men and women who lead the organizations included in this study are also generally known to hold strong moral scruples and have a good sense for the ethical issues relevant to their business operations. In short, they are perceived as really caring about business ethics.

And finally, the ethical leaders observed are empathic. They show an ability to recognize and sympathize with the views and concerns that various parties might hold with respect to specific company actions. They are also aware of the risks that people at lower levels in the organizatino can run in taking ethical stances. For example, when an operating unit's profits are down significantly from forecasted levels during a time of lagging corporate performance, the fact that the recall of a defective product or the elimination of dangerous working conditions was the reason for the shortfall might well be overlooked in faulting the operating managers unless ethical considerations are truly honored in the company. In the words from Hewlett-Packard's statement of corporate objectives, "employees [must] have faith in the motives and integrity of their peers, managers, and the company itself." A person's ability to inspire such faith in others is the stuff of ethical leadership.

There are some who believe that having ethical people in an organization is the one, fundamental condition necessary for having an ethical corporation. This assessment might be correct for a company of saints. But with the frailty of human nature and the powerful pressures for financial performance in today's competitive world of business, it would be folly for corporate leaders to rely on this one dimension. To secure corporate ethical behavior, senior managers must do more. They need to provide moral leadership by their commitment to business ethics and by their sensitivity and responsiveness to critical moral issues connected with corporate activities. They need to provide sound strategic and operational leadership so that the organizational units are able to achieve acceptable performance goals in an ethical manner. And they need to provide a structure of policies, procedures, and practices that encourage ethical behavior and discourage improper conduct.

But just as it would be a mistake for senior management to focus attention solely on the moral character of employees to the exclusion of these other factors, so too would it be a mistake to overlook its importance. Having ethical people is not something that happens automatically or that management can take for granted. This asset has to be deliberately developed and carefully nurtured as part of a long-term effort to manage corporate ethics. Senior management does this by recruiting people with strong moral convictions and rejecting candidates lacking in this respect. It does this by helping employees to connect their personal values to their work functions. And it does this by rewarding ethical behavior and placing people skillful in providing moral leadership in positions where such leadership can have the greatest effect.

6

Elevating the Ethical Character of the Firm

In introducing or elevating ethical standards of organizational behavior, senior management faces a number of added difficulties
when compared to managing corporate ethics as an ongoing process. One is the need to *change* people's thinking and behavior
rather than just preserve the habits and commitments of an organization already accustomed to established ethical standards. They
must learn what is expected of them and the reasons for the new
goals. They have to feel reassured that the changes are in their best
interest, or at least not to their disadvantage. And they have to
develop new attitudes and habits. Another likely difficulty is a
need to introduce or adapt organizational structures, policies, and
practices in support of the new or heightened ethical standards.
Management must identify what needs to be added, eliminated, or
changed. It must also deal with such considerations as timing (how
quickly to act), priorities (in what order), and emphasis (where does
management devote its efforts). A need to strengthen and adapt
managerial skills and judgment so as to conform with redefined
corporate ethical concerns can present yet another difficulty.

Earlier chapters, for the most part, examined how corporate
ethics is managed as an ongoing process. In the one case describing
an attempt to revitalize and upgrade a company's commitment to
ethical standards (Chapter 2), we read how CSI's corporate managers made serious mistakes in failing to clearly define their objec-

tives, adopting an industry-model approach to business ethics without attempting to tailor it to the organization's particular needs, and imposing the new policies and procedures from the top without letting the people affected contribute to the process. These failings are instructive as to what senior managers need to do in support of the desired change process. First, they must make clear to themselves and others their concerns and intentions. Then they must devote time and resources to gain a full understanding of the ethical issues relevant to the firm and develop appropriate policies and practices for motivating desired behavior. Finally, when the necessary groundwork has been laid, they must push responsibility for these matters down to the operating levels where the desired attitudes and behavior are to function in the normal course of business.

These three considerations might seem obvious to the reader. They are not so obvious in practice. Rather, as corporate experiences of a related nature indicate, the process of change is more likely to be haphazard and forced, often in response to trauma or frustration, than orderly and planned.[1] The story of Texas Instruments' experiences in revitalizing and upgrading corporate ethical standards gives an uncommon example of orderly development.

Texas Instruments

In its efforts to raise operational commitment to ethical behavior, senior management at Texas Instruments moved in a deliberate and appropriate manner. Each of the three considerations for increasing organizational understanding and involvement was handled in an effective manner.

Making Clear Senior Management's Concerns and Intentions

Steeped in a rich tradition of technical achievement and business success, Texas Instruments (TI) also prides itself on its ethical conduct. It is still common to hear senior TIers refer to founders Eric Jonsson and Cecil Green as persons whose moral values were beyond reproach. In 1987, Jerry R. Junkins, then president and chief executive officer and soon to become chairman, opened his statement about ethics on this note.

> TI's reputation for integrity—for honesty, fairness, candor and respect in all business dealings—dates back to the founders of the

company. That reputation is a priceless asset. A large part of the pride we all feel in working at TI comes from knowing that this company is respected for its ethical behavior.

On the question of priorities between the firm's aggressive business goals and its strong moral stand, Pat Haggerty, a driving force in TI's early years, is remembered as saying, "We want to play the game and use the whole field, but I don't want to see chalk on either shoe."

By the mid-1980s, senior management began to sense a growing need to revisit and possibly revitalize the company's traditional approach for ensuring acceptable ethical conduct. The impetus for this growing concern came from pressures originating both outside and inside the firm.

External Pressures

The defense industry gained much notoriety in the early 1980s as the number and seriousness of allegations concerning procurement irregularities and other illegal actions mounted in the press. In mid-1985, President Reagan asked David Packard, chairman of Hewlett-Packard and a former deputy secretary of defense, to chair an independent Blue Ribbon Commission on Defense Management that would look into the problems and make recommendations for improvement. As one of the nation's major defense contractors, TI recognized its vulnerability to growing public discontent and to any broad legislative measures that might be taken to counter further abuse.

The Packard Commission, apprehensive about the limitations of federal regulation, recommended self-governance as the principal means for curbing industry misconduct. In the late spring of 1986, representatives of 18 large defense contractors met and drafted six principles for promoting ethical business conduct that became known as the Defense Industry Initiatives on Business Ethics and Conduct, or DII. (See Exhibit 6-1.) The leadership of TI agreed with the prevailing notion of self-regulation and favored the principal measures proposed by DII.[2] These measures not only called for certain specific actions but also encouraged a broad self-examination of ethical standards and the means for achieving them.

Internal Pressures

Management's interest in reexamining ethical behavior was also prompted in part by the company's considerable growth in size. A

1. Each company will have and adhere to a written code of business ethics and conduct.

2. The company's code establishes the high values expected of its employees and the standard by which they must judge their own conduct and that of their organization; each company will train its employees concerning their personal responsibilities under the code.

3. Each company will create a free and open atmosphere that allows and encourages employees to report violations of its code to the company without fear of retribution for such reporting.

4. Each company has the obligation to self-govern by monitoring compliance with federal procurement laws and adopting procedures for voluntary disclosure of violations of federal procurement laws and corrective actions taken.

5. Each company has a responsibility to each of the other companies in the industry to live by standards of conduct that preserve the integrity of the defense industry.

6. Each company must have public accountability for its commitment to these principles.

Exhibit 6–1 Principles of the Defense Industry Initiative

(*Source:* "Conduct and Accountability, A Report to the President by the President's Blue Ribbon Commission on Defense Management," June 1986, p. 42)

former senior vice president in the Defense Systems and Electronics Group (DSEG), expressed the problem as follows.

> When I joined TI in 1962, the whole company had about 18,000 people. I now have over 6,500 people reporting to me. The day after I was hired, I spent several hours with the top person, and the one thing I remember was being told, "You do not have to make deals with anybody requiring you to lie, cheat, or steal. You just walk out." As we get bigger, how can I have the same impact so that the guy who walks in the door will still remember what I said 26 years later?

Sam Self, group controller for DSEG, gave some idea as to the nature of the difficulty by depicting the organizational hierarchy with a triangle.

> At the top is Jerry Junkins. Our group president and the DSEG vice presidents know Jerry and understand what is acceptable and what is not acceptable. The hundred or so program managers at the next level know the vice presidents and get a fairly good idea what these limits are and what behavior is expected. But as you drop down

to the first line supervisors and finally to the 23,000 "doers," there is less and less understanding of what is acceptable.

This comment referred only to one group in the company. For TI as a whole, the number of people involved was three times greater.

Actions taken in response to severe business problems during the late 1970s and early 1980s further weakened organizational confidence in TI's true commitment to integrity and respect for employees. The after-effects were still evident years later, as in the following comment by a senior manager. "We had some massive layoffs, involving 2,000 to 3,000 people. Despite efforts to ease the pain, the company hurt a lot of people. We look at that as a failure." And although no one reported "chalk on either shoe," several executives described as excessive the pressure that group management for semiconductors had put on its organization at the time to improve performance.

Faced with mounting industry attention to ethics, with the need to adapt its ethical legacy to the requirements of a vastly larger organization, and with recent actions that undermined employee trust in management, TI's senior managers held frequent discussions all through 1986 to consider possible actions that might strengthen the organization's commitment to basic ethical values. These discussions enabled senior managers to clarify their understanding of the challenge TI faced and to develop a common resolve for action. In early 1987, the decision was made to establish an Ethics Office as a "clearing house" for ethics issues, with responsibility for building the organization's ethical awareness.

Understanding Issues and Developing Appropriate Policies and Practices

Senior management's initial resolve for improving ethical conduct requires additional learning both about the nature of the challenge and the skills and methods for promoting organizational commitment. The selection of appropriate staff support, a proper definition for the staff role, adequate time, and senior management involvement are critical to this effort. TI did well on all these counts.

TI Ethics Director

The person selected to serve as TI's first ethics director was Carl Skooglund, a vice president who had first joined Texas Instruments in 1965 following employment with Westinghouse. Over the years, he assumed various responsibilities in research and operations, serving as manager of a digital logic integrated circuit department and manager of TI's materials division. In 1985, Skooglund was given responsibility for directing a program to promote quality consciousness and commitment in TI's Semiconductor Group. This job exposed him to a number of the company's operating units and required an ability on his part to obtain cooperation from busy people at all levels of the organization. His success in leading this effort made him an obvious candidate for the job of ethics director. A friendly, easy-going, principled, and ingenuous person, Skooglund is well liked. Imaginative and well organized, he is also widely respected.

Appointed TI Ethics Director in May 1987, Skooglund reports to an Ethics Committee which in turn reports to the Audit Committee of the board of directors. Skooglund's supporting staff includes a manager, highly experienced in communications and training, and a secretary.

Role of the Ethics Director

Concurrent with the official announcement of Carl Skooglund's appointment as Ethics Director, Junkins delivered a statement on ethics that was videotaped for distribution throughout TI. Following the reference to traditional channels for dealing with ethical issues—a person's immediate supervisor, higher levels of management, and the corporate legal department—it described the special role the new Ethics Director would play in the future.

> We recently added a fourth channel that is very significant—the TI Ethics Director. TIers with questions or concerns regarding ethical conduct should use this confidential channel to bring issues to the attention of TI management. This will enable TIers to get their questions answered and enable TI management to take whatever action is necessary to be sure TI's ethical standards are being met.

In his role as a confidential channel, Skooglund was free to serve as an intermediary between corporate and operating managements during the sensitive transition period. He began by giving voice to the organization through various means. The starting point for Skooglund was to find out how TI employees perceived ethics and the kinds of issues that concerned them. To obtain this information, he engaged consultants experienced in employee communications to conduct focus group inquiries. Six groups of eight to twelve TI employees each met for two hours to respond to open-ended as well as directed questions. (Two additional groups of employees from other local electronics firms were included for reference purposes.)

The key findings were both comforting and troubling to Skooglund. The positive points included:

- TIers are proud of their company. They feel good about TI's high standards.
- Employees believe that top management considers both short-term and long-term needs.
- No overall, pervasive rule-bending was highlighted by the focus groups.
- Employees want to do the right thing.
- Ethics is viewed as an extension of values—"common sense right or wrong . . . the way we were brought up."

Potential problem areas included a lack of awareness and even of interest in ethical matters:

- There is little concern about the topic of business ethics.
- Acceptance of top managers as effective leaders, but low awareness of their views.
- Employees identify middle managers, sales and marketing people, and financial people as those most likely to create the pressures which lead to rule-bending—most notably the need to bring in new business and to deliver it on time, within budget.
- Engineers rely on procedures, counting on the system to catch any failure or rule-bending.
- Some employees believe their jobs do not involve ethical decisions.
- Almost all non-exempts reject the idea that they play any role in ethical behavior at TI.
- The idea of ethics training per se is often rejected. Some feel it is unnecessary (again, relying on systems), unteachable (there is no way to address every contingency), and irrelevant (TI has no ethics problem).

For Skooglund, another important source of information about employee concerns is the ethics office communications network. This network permits employees to communicate directly with him in one of three ways: (1) a toll-free telephone line with an easy-to-remember number, (800) 33-ETHIC; (2) a secured computer message terminal command; and (3) a special post office box. Con-

"TI has a long-standing tradition of excellence in the ethical conduct of our business. TI has established the Ethics Office to help TIers understand what is needed to continue this tradition.

I'm available to discuss any questions or concerns you have relating to business policies or practices at TI."

Carl Skooglund

Carl Skooglund
TI Ethics Director

To contact Carl:
(Confidentiality or anonymity at your request)

☐ **(800) 33-ETHIC**
Toll-free from anywhere in U.S.

☐ **MSG ETHICS**
(see T ETHIC for assistance)

☐ **TI Ethics Director**
P.O. Box 830801   Richardson, Texas   75083-0801

Exhibit 6–2 Ethics office poster

fidentiality is stressed, as indicated in the following publicity for the computer linkage. "It cannot be traced, no hard copy is printed out, the transmission does not appear on the terminal's log, and the message can go to only one terminal—one that sits on the Ethics Director's desk."

The Ethics Office communication network was actively promoted throughout the company in various ways. To help personalize the service, posters showing Carl Skooglund were widely distributed. (See Exhibit 6-2.) More than a quarter of the 300 inquiries logged during the first two years of the program raised questions about the ethics of particular situations and about TI's policies.

In late 1988, the Ethics Office mailed an eight-page printed ethics awareness survey to the homes of 2,700 TI employees. The recipients were selected on a statistical sampling basis. The purposes of the survey were listed in the following order of priority: (1) a diagnostic instrument to help focus communications efforts; (2) a baseline for tracking change over time; (3) a larger database for validating earlier findings; and (4) another means for raising awareness among respondents. Excerpts from the survey questionnaire are contained in Exhibit 6-3. According to Skooglund, the returns showed increased awareness about ethical issues in connection with TI affairs but otherwise generally confirmed earlier findings.

Adequate Time
While eager to press forward, senior management recognized the need to take its time in making the kind of changes it wanted in an organization as large and complex as TI. Skooglund clearly perceived the priority for doing the job right over doing it quickly. The continuation of the surveying effort almost 18 months into the schedule gives some indication of the measured pace taken. At the same time, he began early to dovetail training and other activities pertaining to organizational involvement into the learning phase so as not to lose the enthusiasm and momentum that senior management had generated at the outset.

Senior Management Involvement in Learning
Senior managers participated in the design of the ethics program and as a matter of course were fully informed of its progress. They reviewed the results of the surveys and received regular feedback from Skooglund concerning problems he faced and his plans of action. Their practice of working out the sticky issues that Skooglund passed on to them for resolution provided a powerful learning experience. Some of these issues forced fresh thinking about existing practices, some introduced new areas of concern into their thinking. Top management's timely and considered responses to employees' concerns and to other unanticipated issues served as powerful reinforcements to its initial announcement of heightened commitment to business ethics.

— 1a ————————————————————————————————

In general, how good is your understanding of TI's ethical standards?

	Very Poor			Fair		Very Good	
	1	2	3	4	5	6	7

KP1

— 1d ————————————————————————————————

To the extent that you are able to determine, how well does TI live up to these ethical standards on a daily basis?

	Not at All			Somewhat		Totally	
	1	2	3	4	5	6	7

KP4

— 5 ————————————————————————————————

Thinking about TIers in the following job functions, how would you rate the ethical choices they generally make on the job in terms of TI's ethical standards?

	Low Ethical Standards			Moderate Ethical Standards		High Ethical Standards		
Engineers	1	2	3	4	5	6	7	KP22
Financial Control	1	2	3	4	5	6	7	KP23
Marketing	1	2	3	4	5	6	7	KP24
Manufacturing	1	2	3	4	5	6	7	KP25
Middle managment	1	2	3	4	5	6	7	KP26
Officers and top executives	1	2	3	4	5	6	7	KP27
Office and clerical	1	2	3	4	5	6	7	KP28
Personnel	1	2	3	4	5	6	7	KP29
Purchasing	1	2	3	4	5	6	7	KP30
Quality Control	1	2	3	4	5	6	7	KP31
Security	1	2	3	4	5	6	7	KP32
Technicians	1	2	3	4	5	6	7	KP33
Your immediate supervisor	1	2	3	4	5	6	7	KP34

— 7 ————————————————————————————————

The following questions are intended to determine if certain situations should be of concern to TI as a corporation. For each situation, there is a series of three questions to be answered. Please circle one number for each of the three questions.

Situation 1: A TIer uses illegal drugs at home.

A. To what extent should TI be concerned about this issue?

Not Concerned At All 1   2   3   4   5   6   7 Very Concerned   KP36

B. To what extent do you think that TI would handle situations like this fairly?

Unfairly 1   2   3   4   5   6   7 Fairly   KP37

C. What is the extent of your knowledge of TI's policy in regard to situations like this?

No Knowledge 1   2   3   4   5   6   7 Very Knowledgeable KP38

Exhibit 6–3 Excerpts from the 1988 TI ethics survey

Listed below are some situations that require ethical decisions. We are interested in what you think TI employees would do. Circle the number that most closely corresponds to how often you believe TI employees would exhibit the stated behavior.

A. Overstate facts on an employment application.

	Never		Sometimes		Very Frequently		
1	2	3	4	5	6	7	KP52

B. Conceal a cost overrun that makes him/her look bad.

	Never		Sometimes		Very Frequently		
1	2	3	4	5	6	7	KP53

If you should happen to discover an ethical problem (i.e., a violation of TI's standards of conduct by someone else) at work, how likely are you to discuss it with:

	Never		Sometimes		Almost Always		
A. A friend at work?	1	2	3	4	5	6	7	KP65
B. Your supervisor?	1	2	3	4	5	6	7	KP66
C. Your personnel administrator?	1	2	3	4	5	6	7	KP67
D. The TI Ethics Director?	1	2	3	4	5	6	7	KP68
E. A Higher manager in your division?	1	2	3	4	5	6	7	KP69
F. Someone outside TI (close friend or family member)?	1	2	3	4	5	6	7	KP70
G. TI Legal Department?	1	2	3	4	5	6	7	KP71
H. The person involved?	1	2	3	4	5	6	7	KP72

In your opinion, how important is it for TI to maintain an Ethics Office?

	Very Unimportant		No Opinion		Vitally Important		
1	2	3	4	5	6	7	KP83

Gaining Organizational Involvement and Commitment

As is true for most large companies, TI already had in place an elaborate set of mechanisms for defining acceptable business conduct and for ensuring compliance. Policies and procedures applying to a wide range of ethics-related issues could be found in its Standard Policies and Procedures Manual and its Personnel Manual. The most important of these were referenced in a 24-page booklet entitled "Ethics in the Business of TI" that had been first published in 1961 and revised in 1968, 1977, 1987, and again in 1990. Similarly, compliance measures were already largely operational in established auditing procedures and normal management oversight practices.

However, no matter how good these established policies and practices might be, senior management has to take actions that signal change to the status quo and encourage increased standards of behavior. These efforts to build widespread commitment in TI included inspirational exhortations, training, and publication of supporting materials.

Inspirational Words

Junkins and other senior executives took every opportunity to explain and promote TI's heightened attention to business ethics. Particularly noteworthy was the corporate-wide distribution of a videotape announcing the new ethical initiative. On it, Junkins reconfirms TI's commitment to "conduct its business in accordance with the highest ethical and legal standards" and charges all employees with this responsibility.

> Let there be no mistake: We will not let the pursuit of sales, billings, or profits . . . distort our ethical principles. We always have, and we always will place integrity before shipping, before billings, before profits, before anything. If it comes down to a choice between making a desired profit and doing it right, you don't have a choice. You'll do it right. We must do it right, in every detail. Expedient compromises or shortcuts for near-term gains are not acceptable.
>
> Resolving a conflict concerning ethical conduct is a matter of personal responsibility. No one should be expected—or permitted—to act in a way that violates his or her personal integrity. Each of you has not only the right but the obligation, to question and seek clarification of ethical issues arising in the workplace. You must pursue any questionable situation until you are satisfied that you fully

The TI Commitment

Mission

Texas Instruments exists to create, make, and market useful products and services to satisfy the needs of customers throughout the world.

Principles

We will accomplish this with "Excellence in everything we do"

- Perform with unquestionable ethics and integrity
- Achieve customer satisfaction through total quality
- Be a world-class technology/manufacturing leader
- Provide profitable growth/fair return on assets
- Achieve continuous improvement with measurable progress
- Be a good corporate citizen

Values

We expect the highest levels of performance and integrity from our people. We will create an environment where people are valued as individuals and treated with respect and dignity, fairness and equality. We will strive to create opportunities for them to develop and reach their full potential and to achieve their professional and personal goals.

TEXAS
INSTRUMENTS

Exhibit 6–4 The TI Commitment

understand the situation, that you understand the appropriate TI policy—and that TI policy is being applied correctly.

Another significant event among senior management's efforts to inspire organizational commitment was the issuance in 1988 of a statement describing TI's mission, operating principles, and values (see Exhibit 6-4). Its appearance approximately a year after the initial launching of the ethics program reflected the lengthy deliberations by top level corporate managers as to the makeup and wording of this statement.

Training

Soon after taking responsibility as TI's Ethics Director, Skooglund introduced a training program for salaried employees in the company's defense businesses. A three-hour presentation explained the reasons for the new Ethics Office, pointed out the relevance of ethical concerns for all employees, reviewed the contents of the "Ethics in the Business of TI" publication, and reminded participants about the Ethics Office communication lines. Approximately

12,300 salaried employees attended one of the 53 seminar sessions that Skooglund and senior managers from TI's defense businesses conducted in various company locations from mid-1987 through the end of 1988. As this program drew to a close, the Ethics Office began to offer a series of training sessions for non-exempt employees in defense business units, focusing on issues that technical and manufacturing people were likely to confront. This 90-minute program was organized to permit the operating units themselves to run the training session. Some 25,000 to 30,000 eligible employees participated in the program during the next several years. In 1993, plans were underway to offer a refresher round of training.

Published Materials Promoting Ethics

In late 1988, the Ethics Office published and distributed 40,000 booklets containing 16 of the most pertinent questions and answers about ethical concerns that had emerged from employee communications with the Ethics Office. According to Skooglund, the idea for this publication came from Junkins, who saw a benefit in making this information known to the TI community at large. The resulting ten-page glossy booklet also furnished five tear-out wallet cards for an easy reference to TI's ethical guidelines. (The two sides of a card are reproduced in Exhibit 6-5.)

In early 1989, the Ethics Office distributed communications sourcebooks to all TI persons in a position to give the ethics message to people inside and outside the company. The recipients included all managers through department level, publication editors, training and recruiting personnel, salespersons, speechwriters, public relations and advertising specialists, and all public speakers.

TI Ethics Office 800•33•ETHIC	**TI Ethics Office 800•33•ETHIC**
ETHICS QUICK TEST	**WHERE TO GO FOR ETHICS ANSWERS:**
• Is the action **legal**?	• Talk with your supervisor.
• Does it comply with our **values**?	• Contact the Personnel Department.
• If you do it, will you feel **bad**?	• Use the Open Door.
• How will it look in the **newspaper**?	• Call the Legal Department.
• If you know it's **wrong**, don't do it!	• Contact the Ethics Office.
• If you're not sure, **ask**.	
• Keep asking until you get an **answer**.	

Exhibit 6–5 TI Ethics Office wallet card

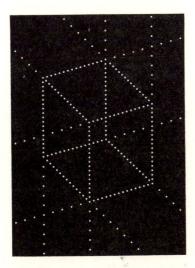

Exhibit 6–6 The Cornerstone

The introduction explained the reason for the three-ring binder "idea book."

> TIers will be hearing much about ethics—through supplemental brochures, posters, videos, and meetings. But the message of sound ethics must continue to appear first and foremost as a natural part of working at TI.
>
> In short, the most important and meaningful way for TIers to receive the word on TI's commitment to the proper conduct of business is through you, the communicator. Because your communications are a normal part of TI. . . . Just like good ethics.

Paralleling this effort to thread the ethics message unobtrusively into normal communications was another to provide ethics with a distinctive symbol that would "break away" from normal company literature and result in stronger recognition of the ethics message. For this purpose the "Cornerstone" was selected and portrayed as shown in Exhibit 6-6. A booklet with the cornerstone word and graphic on its cover explained this choice of symbol. "What is a cornerstone? The most important part of any foundation. The base on which everything else stands. At Texas Instruments, a cornerstone of our business is ethics, sound ethical principles have made us what we are . . . ."

This booklet featured questions and answers touching on a wide variety of ethical topics of practical interest to TI employees.

Subsequent issues of the *Cornerstone* focused attention on specific areas of ethical concerns: gifts, travel, entertainment (published in 1989); employee and employer rights (1990); U.S. defense business (1991); and ethical leadership (1992). The following questions are illustrative of the coverage:

- How does TI feel about employees using drugs?
- A supplier in another part of the country has invited me to check out a piece of new equipment at his plant. I really can't justify the expense, so the supplier offered to pay for the trip. Is this okay?
- Many airlines, hotels, and rental car companies have Frequent Traveler programs through which I can receive free trips, car rentals, or hotel stays for my personal use through credits that I accumulate as a result of TI business travel. Does TI permit me to do this?
- A local company has asked me to work for them in my spare time doing some computer programming. Does this conflict with TI policy?
- Would my job status be affected if I sent a letter to the local newspaper contesting a TI policy or practice?
- A long-time personal friend has recently taken an influential job in a DoD agency with which TI does business. Our families often spend time together during the Christmas holidays and exchange gifts. How should I handle this?

The success of this format led Skooglund to feature weekly ethics articles via TI's worldwide electronics newspaper. In promoting this communication, the *Ethics Tool Box*, a booklet that provides an overview of all organized sources of ethical information for TI employees, states: "These articles address a variety of subjects, from current hot issues to general information, from answers to inquiries on the communications lines to advice and information on TI ethics." A collection of past articles, entitled *Instant Experience*, is also available from the ethics office to enable TI employees to learn just what the ethical issues and questions have been over the past few years.

By 1993, TI's efforts to raise employees' commitment to high standards of ethical behavior generally was acknowledged as successful work-in-progress. Interestingly, the principal source of initial success also carried seeds of possible erosion. According to Skooglund, the strong management involvement in the corporate ethics program raised the expectations of many employees to an excessive level, thereby opening the door to disappointment when these expectations were unmet. In many cases, the reason for disappointment was in getting from the ethics director the same answer or advice that the employee's first-line supervisor had given. In Skooglund's view, employees' increasing familiarity with TI's ethical standards and their growing awareness of the positive effects on organizational climate over time would revive on a firmer basis much of the earlier enthusiasm.

Change Process for Corporate Ethics

While circumstances are bound to differ among individual companies, TI's approach for increasing organizational commitment to ethical behavior provides a sound base model for general use. Top management's resolve to elevate the ethical character of the firm is a critical first step. Since the necessary understanding of what issues to address and how important they are normally grows over time with discussion and experience, it is especially important for senior managers to keep an open mind during this stage. To prevent employees from misinterpreting open mindedness as confusion or lack of direction, top management must take care to demonstrate firm resolve with respect to broad purpose while leaving room to learn and adapt with respect to specific issues and actions.

The next step is for senior management to define the objectives of the ethics program, develop appropriate policies and practices, and coordinate the various efforts. Many companies make the mistake of imitating what one or more firms with reputations for business ethics appear to be doing or say they are doing. One problem with this approach is that critical design considerations are not necessarily visible and consequently can be overlooked. Moreover, the task of starting or ramping-up an ethics program is sufficiently difficult and individual firms sufficiently different so as to make direct imitation generally of little worth and sometimes even counterproductive.

Finally, responsibility for ensuring organizational compliance and commitment needs to be pushed down through organizational ranks. This delegation is critically important to creating a motivating force capable of permeating an entire organization. The operating line managers are in the best position to adopt and adapt procedures for specific business operations. Moreover, as we have seen, an employee's direct boss often plays a key role in setting the moral tone for the work environment.

While this approach might appear straightforward, and perhaps even easy, such impressions are far from being correct, as the following evaluation of General Dynamics Corporation's efforts to mount an ethics program reveals.

Turning Around Ethically Troubled Firms

In mid-1985, Secretary of the Navy John Lehman suspended contracts at two General Dynamics divisions because of overcharges on defense contracts, canceled two missile contracts worth $22.5 million, and fined the company $676,283 for giving presents to Admiral Hyman Rickover while he directed the navy's Trident submarine program.[3] The following day, the company announced that its chairman and chief executive officer, David Lewis, would retire by the end of the year. The vice chairman of TRW, Stanley Pace, who was nicknamed "Mr. Clean" in the press, was selected to replace Lewis. One of the first actions of the chairman-to-be was to commission a corporate-wide Ethics Program with the specific objective of putting the Standards of Business Ethics and Conduct into practice.

On the surface, the subsequent efforts at General Dynamics to put the standards of business ethics and conduct into practice appear to mirror those at TI. As a staff member involved in the implementation of the Ethics Program in the Electronics Division reported,[4]

> The plan was implemented in four phases: (a) a high-level planning meeting, (b) appoint division-level Ethics Directors, (c) appoint internal trainers and prepare them, and (d) train all employees in the organization in the standards and expectations.
>
> • • •
>
> The training sessions were four hours long for salaried, professional employees, and two hours long for all other employees. In addition to covering the rules, the training session was designed to heighten employees' awareness of common ethical dilemmas and how to deal with them.
>
> • • •
>
> In [1985] the Board of Directors established the Committee on Corporate Responsibility to review the effectiveness of the Ethics Program and to receive reports on its progress. In addition to the Committee, the Chairman and Chief Executive Officer created the Corporate Ethics Steering Group to provide advice on the implementation of the program. The Steering Group reviewed policies, proce-

dures, and practices and made recommendations for improvements. The Steering Group was composed of corporate functional heads including Legal, Human Resources, Internal Audit, Contracts and Pricing, International Offset, and Controller.

• • •

In addition to their training, the scope and gravity of the Ethics Program was communicated to all employees in various articles in company newspapers.

Moreover, according to the same source, the Ethics Director for General Dynamics was generally acknowledged to be a highly competent manager of unquestionable integrity.

A group of five administrators who had had firsthand experience in the Electronics Division with planning and implementing the Ethics Program (referred to as the planning group) agreed "that the program was properly planned, that commitment from top managers was strong, that the organization for administration of the program was appropriate, and that communication of the program objectives was adequate."

Despite these appropriate inputs, evaluations of the results were mixed. On the one hand, the Ethics Program was judged effective and successful in getting employees to follow rules and standards of conduct. As evidence, "the planning group . . . cited high usage of the various channels for complaints and inquiries, high levels of employee trust in the program, fair and timely investigations and appropriate corrective actions, and new employee attitudes towards customer and public relations. Three respondents pointed out that the company had not been involved in the latest sweeping scandals involving government contractors. Government officials tend to support the claim that the Ethics Program at General Dynamics was successful."[5] Also put forward was the view that the Ethics Program had become permanent and would not be discarded without serious repercussions.

On the other hand, a group of ten salaried professional employees and five hourly employees who had been selected to provide an employees' perception of the Ethics Program were highly critical of the results.

> The . . . group unanimously agreed that the program did not live up to their personal expectations. Shortfalls cited were in the areas of being treated with respect by supervisors, being listened to by management, supervisory responsibility to employees, company programs to reward employees, and open and honest communication between supervisors and employees and between departments.

• • •

Twelve of the 15 members felt the program was a sham, and
that it was "simply a whitewash scheme to present a false front to
(the government)." The remaining three members could probably be
best characterized as neutral rather than positive about the program.
They unanimously agreed that the program did nothing to promote
the welfare of the employees of the company.[6]

The study also noted that many employees had indicated their reluctance to report on possible unethical actions for fear of reprisals.

According to these findings, the Ethics Program clearly failed
in one important respect: "General Dynamics executives were un-
successful in building trust between themselves and their employees."[7] The study sheds light on some important possible reasons
for this failure. To start, General Dynamics had not had a tradition
of concern for its employees. In 1986, "less than one-third of
corporate-wide survey respondents rated their division managers as
good or very good on taking a genuine interest in their welfare.
And only about one-quarter of corporate-wide respondents felt the
organization had a cooperative atmosphere."[8] Not surprisingly, senior managers were reluctant to change the sharply delineated
power structure of the firm's three-tier organizational hierarchy,
comprising executives, professional and administrative, and non-
exempt workers. Consequently, pressures for changes were almost
entirely from external sources and concerned primarily the company's business dealings with external parties.

Several factors constrained the new chairman from dealing effectively with the ethical issues relating to how employees were to
be regarded and treated in General Dynamics. As an outsider, Pace
did not have first-hand experience with the corporate culture. His
likely short tenure, given his earlier-announced plans to retire from
TRW, further weakened his leverage for altering management's attitudes and relationships. And perhaps most significant, the immediate task before him was to regain General Dynamics' good standing with the U.S. Navy and to reestablish a favorable public image.

Exacerbating the situation were employees' perceptions of having been duped by the company in its efforts to obtain their support
for the Ethics Program. The basic document offered "to make the
work environment more conducive to individual dignity and mutual respect, and to promote fair treatment of employees by their
managers and supervisors."[9] Accordingly, "[e]mployees expected
increased concern for their welfare by their managers, increased
humanistic treatment by their superiors, and increased levels of

their own participation in work-related decisions."[10] However, three years later, the fraction of employees who reported that management was interested in their ideas and opinions had still remained at the 1986 level of only about one-third.

Strong staff leadership and administration resulted in a program that achieved top management's limited goals. Staff efforts to broaden the definition of ethical behavior—as implied by Kent Druyvesteyn, Staff Vice President-Ethics Program, when he announced, "The purpose of the General Dynamics Ethics Program is to help employees in their everyday business activity, not to catch them in wrongdoing" and as further revealed in the published list of "lessons learned" contained in Exhibit 6-7—were frustrated by senior line managers reluctant to change and consequently largely ineffective.[11] The ten lessons would provide valuable guidelines for any company that desires greater organizational commitment to ethical behavior. Reportedly, they were largely ignored at General Dynamics and viewed as window dressing for outsiders to see.

In light of this and other evidence, the study concluded that the concepts of mutual respect and fair treatment were "primarily a sales ploy to encourage people to follow the rules."[12] It accused the company of raising employees' expectations unrealistically with the idea that being ethical would enhance the quality of work life when no actual change in work life was intended. The perceived misrepresentation, cited earlier in connection with the employees' evaluation of the Ethics Program, engendered employee resentment and even cynicism. Some respondents were reported to doubt whether senior division managers had actually made ethical behavior a part of their agenda.

General Dynamics versus Texas Instruments

In comparing and contrasting the efforts to promote ethical behavior at Texas Instruments (TI) and General Dynamics (GD), several factors stand out to explain the different outcomes. The most important difference concerned the basic goals of the programs. At GD, senior managers were taking corrective actions in an effort to save their business, and everyone knew it. Texas Instruments was not involved with any pending investigation or indictments. As a result, TI's senior management was relatively unconstrained in the scope of its ethical concerns while GD's was under pressure to correct certain specific categories of improper actions. Moreover, the

1. The average person has a strong personal sense of integrity and guards his or her reputation jealously. This sense is the strength of an ethics program.

2. People often respond emotionally to the word "ethics." Reactions are often negative, defensive, or cynical. The word must be used carefully in building an ethics program.

3. The commitment of all persons in positions of leadership is an absolute condition for establishing an ethics program. But the commitment of all employees at all levels is absolutely necessary to fully implement and maintain the program.

4. An ethics program is best integrated into the existing structure of the organization. It should not stand alone or exist as a mere appendage. A large independent staff and budget are unnecessary and undesirable.

5. The aim of the program must be positive. The program must give help. Its primary purpose is to teach and guide — not catch and judge.

6. The program should focus on questions of right and wrong but not ignore appearances of right and wrong. Appearance may be as damaging to the reputation of the company as fact.

7. Issues that may involve possible questions of ethics arise unexpectedly and often unpredictably. Because there is sometimes little time to decide, a means or method of obtaining emergency assistance is necessary.

8. Most issues of an ethical nature are practical matters of fact. When the relevant facts are gathered, the question is answered and the concern is resolved. Few of the issues faced by employees are real moral dilemmas although they appear to be very perplexing at the moment. Employees do not need to be moral philosophers to solve most ethics-related questions they may face.

9. Many questions of an ethical nature would never arise if communications were stronger in the basic relationships between employer and employee, employee and customer, employee and supplier, employee and shareholder, and employee and community. Likewise, many questions that escalate into issues of ethics would arise less often if common civil virtues like trustworthiness, loyalty, helpfulness, friendliness, courtesy, kindness, cheerfulness, and respect were practiced regularly.

10. An ethics program has certain inherent limitations based on the fact that it depends on people for implementation. There can be written standards and carefully defined policies, but the program can do little to change individuals who intentionally engage in misconduct.

Exhibit 6–7 Ethics program lessons learned

voluntary nature of TI's program provided a more favorable setting for top management to assure employees of its good intentions than was the case at GD.

Texas Instruments' long-standing concern with ethics gave its management another important advantage over GD, where little attention had been paid to such matters. As Skooglund, TI Ethics Director, noted,

> Our approach clearly was to reinforce a long-standing emphasis on ethics. Even in our first ethics book [1961], we emphasized the fact that "the trust and respect of all people . . ." are essential values. Fortunately, this message was in place decades before the Ethics Office and program came into existence. We also have had an open door process for a long time and have emphasized informality and few "status symbols." I believe this helped the credibility of our fairness message.

The author of the GD ethics program evaluation study observed that his former company had come from a much less humanistic tradition regarding the organization's work environment.

General Dynamics also exacerbated its employees' apprehensiveness in a number of ways. For example, violations were routinely summarized by category as well as the sanctions applied. Moreover, GD employees were required to sign a card stating that they had received, read, and understood the requirements. Texas Instruments intentionally chose not to follow such potentially intimidating practices, attempting instead to be supportive in its actions rather than punitive. In this connection, Skooglund observed,

> We have defined ethics as "the expectation and understandings that define how we deal with others. . . ." When we do not meet those expectations the attitude seems to be one of "we're not doing what we say we should do" rather than "the Ethics Program is a sham." In fact, we recently held a cultural audit. One of the statements that people were asked to respond to was "I understand that TI is very serious about ethics." Over seventy percent responded as either "strongly agree" or "very strongly agree."

While TI succeeded in having its ethical program contribute to employees' morale, GD did not. The failure at GD reflected a narrow definition of ethics by senior line managers. Their concern to have the company act correctly in its dealings with customers and suppliers largely ignored the vital issues concerning the work environment. And even within this limited purview, in the opinion of some observers, the company's actions were motivated by pure business needs with no sense of moral obligation.

Broad Lessons

Firms that blatantly disregard ethical behavior as a matter of course clearly face far greater difficulties in developing an ethical corporate culture than TI did. Organizational disinterest, or even disdain, regarding business ethics can pose formidable barriers to change. Pressures for financial performance coupled with minimal controls regarding how goals get accomplished create the playing field for self-serving actions. The resulting corporate culture attracts and rewards employees who share the "anything goes" attitude of senior managers.

For such firms, any real corporate turnaround regarding ethical behavior must start with changes in top management's thinking. This thinking needs to go beyond a willingness for taking measures to avoid scandals and litigation. At the very least, it should encompass a genuine desire to encourage ethical behavior as normal corporate conduct.

For incumbent corporate executives of ethically troubled firms to experience the necessary change in mindset would be an improbable event. And were such to occur, it could take years for employees and outsiders to overcome their suspicions regarding management's true motives. Consequently, as a practical matter, the start of an ethical turnaround for such firms is likely to require replacement of the senior managers who initiated, encouraged, or tolerated unethical behavior with people who have reputations for being ethical business practitioners. A good case in point is the top-level housecleaning that Salomon Brothers experienced in the wake of the bond-trading scandal in 1991. Chief Executive Officer John Gutfreund, Vice Chairman John Meriwether, and President Thomas Strauss were all forced out, and Warren Buffett, one of the nation's leading investors with a reputation for honest dealings as well as a major stake in the company, was put in charge. This one move went a long way to creating positive expectations about the propriety of Salomon Brothers' future business activities.[13]

However, this kind of top management replacement in itself does not necessarily provide the needed moral leadership. The experiences of Texas Instruments and General Dynamics make clear that a business leader's personal integrity and moral commitment, as important as they are, are not sufficient to ensure organizational trust and support. General Dynamics' Stanley Pace probably compares favorably with TI's Jerry Junkins or any of the other people leading the ethical companies studied when it comes to moral values and personal integrity. But the mistakes that he and many other business leaders make in putting forward a business ethics program, unmindful of the many possible causes for suspicion and mistrust, doom their efforts, however sincere and well intentioned they might be. The large investment of resources that Pace devoted to the ethics program at General Dynamics strikingly failed to create the kind of organizational spirit that could provide opportunity for achieving corporate excellence.

7

Engaging the Ethics Supercharger

As should be clear by now, business ethics complicates a manager's life. To compete successfully over time is a difficult enough challenge for most business firms. The constraints that ethical concerns might impose on corporate actions and the added burden of having to confront an organization with complex and potentially divisive moral considerations can make the business challenge that much more difficult. Conceivably, the need to deal with corporate ethics could overwhelm a management inexperienced in such matters and already burdened by stressful business conditions. But to argue against management's trying to achieve corporate ethical behavior on the basis of this risk is somewhat like eschewing physical exercise because it could be harmful to people who are grossly overweight or out of condition. The key consideration in either case is that the effort be sensible, recognizing the party's capacity for change.

This book opens with the implicit question, "Is corporate ethics worth the effort?," and then argues in the affirmative. The costs are easy to see when one considers the amount of time and effort senior managers and others in the organization must devote to promoting ethical behavior. The benefits are also readily apparent. They include: the sense of personal pride and satisfaction that people can derive from being part of a fair-minded organization; the avoidance of costly litigation and crippling scandals; improved corporate relationships with customers, suppliers, investors, and the community at large; and the generation of conditions that favor individual and organizational creativity and initiative. This last item, however, is only a potential benefit. To tap this potential requires another set of policies and practices relating to the management of innovation and risk taking. The ethics supercharger has to be harnessed and exploited.

Johnson & Johnson provides an excellent case in point. The venerable 100-year-old company was featured in the concluding article of a *Wall Street Journal* series on how big companies succeed over time.[1] As evidence of J&J's successful adaptation and innovation, the account presents the following data: of 21 units identified as "principal domestic operations" in 1982, a third have been sold or shut; more than half of such units in 1991 did not exist 10 years earlier; a third of the company's sales come from products introduced in the past five years; revenues have more than doubled, dividends more than tripled, and earnings per share increased an average of 13.3 percent annually over the past decade; and the value of $100 worth of common stock has risen to $460 in the same 10-year period.

The secret of J&J's success is perhaps best captured in the opening paragraph of a statement that had been put forward in 1980 to serve as a guideline for strategic planning.

> We believe the consistency of our overall performance as a corporation is due to our unique form of decentralized management, our adherence to the ethical principles embodied in our Credo, and our emphasis on managing the business for the long term.

As elaborated in the body of this statement, the idea is to make business unit managers responsible for providing specific end users with quality products and services of superior value on a profitable basis over time. (The statement of strategic direction is contained in Exhibit 7-1.)

J&J's 1981 annual report, with its cover highlighting the formula *decentralization = creativity = productivity*, had this to say about the nature and purpose of decentralization.

> Johnson & Johnson is not one company but many. . . . Whatever their size or location, they share a commitment to meeting the special needs of a well-defined customer. In doing so, they create a wide variety of innovative ways to successfully run their businesses.
> We feel that the secret to liberating that productivity is decentralization—granting each company sufficient autonomy to

We believe the consistency of our overall performance as a corporation is due to our unique form of decentralized management, our adherence to the ethical principles embodied in our Credo, and our emphasis on managing the business for the long term.

There are certain basic principles that we are committed to in this regard:

- The responsibility for our success as a corporation rests in the hands of the presidents and managing directors of our companies. Each must assume leadership in every facet of the business, including the definition of strategic plans and providing for management succession.

- We will attempt to organize our businesses based on the clearly focused needs of the end users of our products and services. In many instances business units will be structured around the worldwide franchise philosophy. We will continue, however, to rely on "umbrella" companies to develop local markets for any of our franchises where this appears to be the best way to initiate cost-effective, long-term growth.

- We will seek, where possible, to achieve or maintain a leadership position in our markets of interest. It is recognized that this can only be accomplished through maintaining, over the long term, end benefits superior to our competition. In this regard, we are committed to improving our internal research and development capability, and to utilizing external sources that provide access to new science and technology.

- We are dedicated to exceptionally high growth. To achieve this we must be well-positioned in growth markets, and each management must be aggressively innovative and strive to grow faster than the markets in which it competes.

- Each management must know how to invest effectively in future earning power while recognizing that it is easier to reduce profits short term than to increase them long term. We further believe that growth should be financed primarily from earnings. This means our companies must generally make above-average profits to support higher rates of growth.

- Acquisitions are viewed as an appropriate way to achieve the strategic goals of a given company or as a way for the corporation to expand the scope of its current business. Such acquisitions - of products, technologies, or businesses - will be evaluated for growth potential, fit with current or future businesses, management capacity, and economic feasibility. There are no other restrictions on the identification of acquisition candidates.

Corporate management is responsible for providing resources, guidance, leadership, and control of the various business entities within the framework of these principles. Management's most important responsibility is the one it shares with presidents and managing directors in attracting the kind of people who can manage our businesses in the future, providing them with the kind of environment that maximizes their potential and with a system that rewards them appropriately for their accomplishments.

Exhibit 7–1 Johnson & Johnson's statement of strategic direction, 1980

conduct its business without unnecessary constraints. In short, we believe decentralization = creativity = productivity.

Jim Burke, former J&J chairman and chief executive officer, elaborated on the concept.

> The basic concept behind the decentralization philosophy is to try to organize each business around a given market need and a given set of customers. It's easier said than done but that's really it . . . Ethicon is an example of a business that's built around the needs of the surgeon sewing people together . . . and their success is based upon their understanding that what they are is an extension of the skills in the hands of the surgeon. With this approach they built this business out of nothing.[2]

Fueling the innovation process is an annual R&D budget of about $1 billion, supplemented by the expenditure of millions of dollars for buying research and technology developed by others. Consistent with its philosophy of decentralization, the company's research and development activities are conducted almost exclusively within the individual business units.

Complementing J&J's skills in developing new products and markets is its readiness to cut loose failures. Ralph S. Larsen, chairman and chief executive officer, attributes the firm's ability to prune unpromising operations to a process at the executive committee level of continuously reviewing the businesses to make sure that they fit the corporate strategy and are performing.[3] This process, according to Dave Clare (former president and chairman of the executive committee), includes a careful review of each operating unit's strategic plans, with special attention to major problems and programs with respect to both five- and ten-year planning horizons.

Senior management's willingness to back new ideas and its attitude toward failure go a long way in explaining J&J's impressive record of success. The Medipren story characterizes the manner in which initiative and failure are handled.

> When a group of managers in 1986 proposed launching a nonprescription pain reliever containing ibuprofen (rather than aspirin or the key ingredient in Tylenol, acetaminophen), then-Chairman James Burke opposed the idea, arguing that the competition had too great a head start. But he allowed his subordinates to proceed anyway. They launched Medipren—an ibuprofen pain reliever virtually identical to American Home Products Corp.'s Advil and Bristol-Myers's Nuprin—and for a few years tried to out-market the competition. It didn't work.[4]

In July 1992, Johnson & Johnson stopped selling Medipren. According to the executive who had overseen the launch, no one was penalized for the failure, an outcome in keeping with senior management's view that corporate growth necessarily involves backing some losers in the search for winners.

Reference in the statement of strategic direction to "adherence to the ethical principles embodied in our Credo" is a clear reminder of J&J's strong commitment to treat with respect its employees, its customers, and the community at large. The above account reveals how senior managers go about tapping the organization's reservoir of trust and pride to encourage innovation and initiative through the influence of an ethical corporate culture[5] favoring innovation.

Corporate Culture Favoring Innovation

In companies like J&J, Cray Research, and Hewlett-Packard, one quickly senses a pervasive interest in and enthusiasm for new product and new business development. For companies in industries such as electronics and pharmaceuticals, rapid technological changes can give impetus to innovation as a way of corporate life. For most companies, senior management must rely more on internally induced pressures for motivating product innovations and business initiatives.

Managing innovation and corporate renewal is a complex process with its own body of literature. This chapter touches on the subject only insofar as it serves to complete the linkage in this book between ethical behavior and sustained corporate excellence. This linkage, shown in Exhibit 7-2, begins with the coupling of sound corporate and business strategies with ethical behavior to foster an organizational climate marked by respect and trust. This powerful combination contains potential energy for motivating the innovative and risk-taking initiatives that are essential to achieving and sustaining corporate excellence. However, to put this potential energy into productive use, senior management must actively engage the ethics supercharger by putting into play policies and practices conducive to organizational creativity.

The vital role management plays in creating a corporate culture favoring innovation and risk taking is evident in Johnson & Johnson and the following account of Nucor Steel.

Nucor Steel

Nucor Steel, an exemplar of business management that has transformed a backwater metalworking manufacturer into America's seventh largest steel producer in just over 20 years, prides itself as an ethical company.[6] It treats its employees with dignity, offering good wages and steady employment. It provides customers with low cost and high quality products through innovative and efficient manufacturing. And it yields generous returns to its shareholders, among whose ranks number many employees. Nucor serves as a role model for how ailing U.S. manufacturing companies can regain

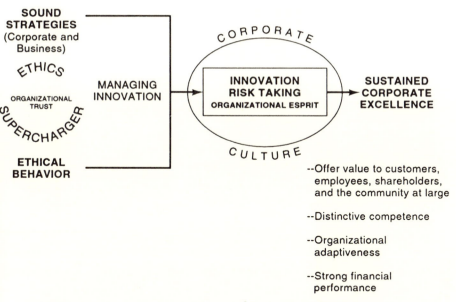

Exhibit 7–2 The ethical supercharger for sustained corporate excellence

their abilities to compete with Japanese and other foreign firms that have all but taken over domestic markets.

Nucor's well-deserved reputation for being one of the most innovative companies in the steel industry in itself reinforces the innovation process. According to F. Kenneth Iverson, chairman and chief executive officer, Nucor's receptivity to new technology encourages suppliers of steel processing equipment and related products from all over the world to approach the firm with their state-of-the-art concepts. Often, with ideas still on the drawing board, Nucor can influence equipment design to suit its particular needs. The company's long history of supporting process innovation also serves to motivate its greatest source of creative ideas—its employees.

One way in which senior management attempts to encourage employees to contribute constructive new ideas is by indicating what is of interest and what is not acceptable. David Aycock, former chief operating officer, made the following observation about Nucor's guidelines for innovative ideas: "We have a simple approach. One, the idea should relate to steel. Two, it should not violate any laws. And three, it cannot be immoral. These rules help us all to avoid wasting time and energy on unacceptable propositions."

Iverson and Aycock had also taken steps to reduce organizational obstructions to the flow of creative ideas in both structure and people. Aycock explained the structural problem: "When a novel idea has to pass through several layers of management for approval, the company has a big problem. None of the intermediary managers can give the OK; any one of them can kill it." The solution to this problem is to give the idea generators direct access to the decision makers. Nucor does this by delegating a high level of authority to the general managers at the plant sites.

To avoid putting the wrong people in positions of authority, Nucor requires all candidates for department head or higher positions to go through two days of psychological testing. Ability to deal with subordinates, adaptability, tolerance for risk, honesty, and integrity are among the desired personality traits. A second line of defense against weak management is in the hands of subordinates. Aycock explained how this works in Nucor. "We have never had a general manager or department head fail for technical shortcomings. The only failures are when they are unable to gain or to hold their employees' confidence and support. The way we look at it, when your employees 'fire' you, you have to go!"

The way in which Nucor's management receives and treats employees' new ideas is another important factor influencing this flow. Aycock explains Nucor's approach.

> We have never said "no" to any employee's idea for creative change. If Ken doesn't like an idea, he might drag his feet a little on the proposal, but if the employee persists, he'll let it go. When times are tough and the company is in a cash bind, we might say that we cannot act now, that the idea should be written up, and that we'll follow up on it when money is available.
>
> The reasons for this positive response are simple. First, almost all of the ideas are very good and we can't always know which ones won't work. One thing that we have learned is that our people don't come forward with dumb ideas. Second, if you discourage one idea, the message you send is that you are also not interested in the next idea.
>
> In my experience, one of the common mistakes in business is not to be supportive enough of new ideas from employee ranks. We believe that it is important to give the "go ahead" and to fund these initiatives.

Iverson's views on decision making help put this approach in perspective. "I'm a great believer in making mistakes. Nothing ventured, nothing gained. The fact of the matter is that good managers make bad decisions. They just ought to make more good decisions than bad."

Aycock also emphasized the importance of management's not second-guessing an employee's idea. In his view, the time for management's suggestions is after a project is underway, not before—unless specifically asked for. And even when requested, as the following interchange illustrates, managers have to remain vigilant against appropriating unintentionally the ideas of their subordinates.

> EMPLOYEE: I've got this idea; but my manager won't listen. Do you want my opinion?
> AYCOCK: No, I don't want your opinion. It's your affair. But maybe you want my opinion.
> EMPLOYEE: (Pause) Yeah, I like that better.

In the space of a few moments, Aycock was able to communicate his interest and support to the employee without taking over ownership of the initiative.

Successful innovations are openly acclaimed at Nucor. However, the rewards do not include cash payments. Aycock explains, "Praise and recognition is easy to share without giving grounds for invidious comparisons. With money, you can easily cause hard feelings and jealousy when people compare awards. The problem is that it is almost impossible in our business for management to know just who contributed to a specific initiative and the relative importance of the various contributions. And even if we could make these assessments, the employees involved wouldn't necessarily agree with us."

One of "the most dangerous situations," according to Aycock, is when there is a realization that an innovative project is failing or has failed. Terminating the effort must be done without embarrassing or otherwise penalizing the advocates. He notes, "Ken and I have to make sure that the organization understands that these people are still corporate heroes, just as are those whose ideas have succeeded. It's the people who do nothing to improve our operations that are not heroes. When a failure occurs, we are on the lookout to discourage anyone from gloating and saying 'I told you so.' "

"The most destructive force with respect to innovation," warns Aycock, "is to make scapegoats of the people involved in a failed initiative. Such self-serving on management's part is not only counterproductive, it is also highly unethical. When management approves a project, it assumes co-responsibility. It should share in the blame—if there is to be blame—as well as in the glory."

As the last comment indicates, ethical considerations are an inextricable part of the innovation process at Nucor. Iverson and Aycock are keenly aware that employees must trust in management's being truly supportive of their efforts, whatever the outcomes, for them to put themselves on the line. While management's ability to engage the ethics supercharger clearly depends on its day-to-day, week-after-week handling of new ideas and initiatives, this task can be greatly eased when the connection between ethics and innovation is anticipated in the firm's strategic long-range planning efforts.

Looking Ahead

The description of ethical firms in Chapter 1 noted that they all are good at avoiding ethical problems wherever possible and at dealing effectively with ethical problems when they arise. The point was also made that the most effective way to deal with ethical problems is not to have them in the first place. As military science demonstrates, early warning of potential troubles provides valuable opportunities for evasion or prepared engagement. This principle also holds true for ethical affairs. Looking and planning ahead are vital to avoiding ethical problems. Making a firm's ethical long-range navigation system an integral part of its normal strategic planning process, when done right, is undoubtedly the most effective way for aligning business operations with the organization's values and ethical aspirations.

Ethics and Strategy

Corporate strategy and business ethics connect in many important ways. Safety and new product design is a good example of an area where ethical foresight can help a corporation avoid future difficulties that not only damage its reputation in the eyes of consumers and of society at large but also undermine organizational trust and confidence in management. One need only consider the many reports of injuries and deaths allegedly resulting from faulty product design of automobiles and small children's toys to imagine how counterproductive the failure to place enough weight on safety when planning new products can be to any corporation yearning for excellence.

Safety in working conditions is another area where ethical foresight can help corporations avoid unnecessary and costly injuries and deaths that can subvert employees' trust in managements' regard for them. In this connection, corporate planning needs to address such forward-looking considerations as plant design (to identify and avoid potential workplace dangers, such as exposure to toxic substances), training and enforcement (to ensure that the company's safety procedures are appropriate for new production operations and for new workers who might differ from the firm's traditional workforce with respect to education, experience, gender, and other important dimensions), and workload scheduling (to anticipate any ramp-up expansion of operations so as to avoid excessive overtime that could prove dangerous). The need to include these issues explicitly and systematically in strategic planning is likely to be greatest for operations located abroad—such as in Mexico, Southeast Asia, or Eastern Europe—where employees' abilities to raise objections are diminished.

When corporate strategic planning addresses organizational development and morale (as it should), a host of topical issues come up for consideration regarding future policies and practices. Current items of this nature would include: child care for employees, diversity in the workforce, sexual harassment, substance abuse, and AIDS.[7]

Possibly the most important connection between strategy and ethics is the effect that business performance can have on ethical behavior. As discussed earlier, senior management's ability to sustain high standards of corporate ethical behavior depends in no small measure on its ability to provide strong business leadership. Lewis E. Burns, president and chief executive officer of Dover Industries, is probably not far off in assessing, "The most unethical behavior in business is poor management." Poor management invariably harms a company's capabilities and reduces its effectiveness. As a firm loses its ability to achieve its economic goals through proper and ethical business conduct, pressures begin to mount for acceptance of less proper and even unethical actions. In more than one firm studied, people spoke of how fears of possible takeover motivated top management to increase markedly the pressures for economic performance.[8] One vice president and general manager of a major operating division vividly described this phenomenon, indicating the intensity of such pressures.

> Our chairman doesn't want to be remembered as the person who lost the company's independence. To keep the stock price up, he has made it clear that it is not enough to be profitable for the year, we have to turn in good profits each quarter. The last manager who didn't make the numbers is no longer with us. There is another general manager who is having some difficulties, and the vultures are flying low. We can certainly sense it.

The elevated pressure might improve results by motivating some operating units to work harder, be smarter, or take greater risks. But when a firm already engages in hard driving operations, the greater likelihood is for this fear-inducing pressure to undermine operational commitment to ethical standards.

Past success is no guarantee of future success. Many of America's premier companies have run into hard times because of management's failure to adapt the firm properly to changing conditions. A good example is Sears, Roebuck & Co., a firm whose early strategies reshaped retailing. By 1988, according to the following accounts, it was conspicuously clear that management had lost its way.

> The company seems to have fallen out of step with America, missing sea changes in demography and consumer tastes that have powered competitors' rapid growth. . . . Turning around Sears' retailing operations is the key to its survival strategy, and that will be a daunting challenge.[9]
>
> • • •
>
> But the picture that emerges . . . is of a century-old, muscle-bound behemoth crushed by its lumbering corporate culture, needing new strategy and probably new management. Sears' half-hearted, clumsy efforts to adapt to a competitive retailing environment reveal an American institution in decline, a textbook example of what happens to any company that settles too comfortably into its market.[10]

In 1990, Sears reported a 40 percent drop in earnings and a $155 million write-off, apparently putting Chairman Edward A. Brennan's job on the line. On June 11, 1992, California's Consumer Affairs Department charged that the state's 72 Sears Tire & Auto Centers had systematically made unnecessary auto repairs. Four days later, New Jersey made similar accusations against six Sears auto centers.[11] Sears senior executives denied that they had ever knowingly approved or endorsed such practices. Countering the disclaimer, *Business Week* reported, "Interviews with 18 current and former auto employees, major-appliance salespeople, and Allstate Insurance agents all reveal an atmosphere in which employees feared getting fired if they didn't meet sales quotas. Some even say they felt pressured to cheat to keep their jobs."[12]

Bold steps—some say desperate—have been taken to downsize and realign the corporate structure.[13] Whether Sears' management eventually turns the company around is not the point. What is at issue is senior management's responsibility for preserving a firm's competitive effectiveness and avoiding troubled situations. Contrast the following reports to those for Sears.

> At H. J. Heinz Co.'s management meeting in Pittsburgh in February 1987, Chairman Anthony J. F. O'Reilly warned his top 100 executives of looming crisis. . . . "We cannot continue with past management practices," O'Reilly said.
>
> That speech—and the big changes that followed—are what separate O'Reilly from a lot of other managers. Heinz's sales were still growing at a 6% to 8% annual pace, and its profit margins were among the healthiest in packaged foods. Yet management was questioning the very methods that, over a decade, had nearly quadrupled profits and more than doubled sales.
>
> After a stem-to-stern review of the company, executives decided that what had carried Heinz through the '80s wasn't going to carry it through the '90s . . . [14]
>
> • • •
>
> "There's complacency in this company," complains Frank Shrontz, the Boeing Company chairman and chief executive officer, as he cajoles and bullies for change and improved performance in what is already one of the world's best-managed companies.[15]

To combat this complacency, Shrontz required Boeing's 100 top executives to visit "world-class" Japanese manufacturing firms. The once-skeptical managers were said to have returned in awe, and a variety of improvements were soon put into effect. The resulting attitude was voiced by Dean Thornton, Boeing Commercial Airplane Group President: "We are dedicated to not doing what IBM, Sears Roebuck, and General Motors have done—which is to get to the top, be the best, and then get fat and lazy."[16]

It takes uncommon business judgment for a senior manager to sense a potential or emerging weakness in a firm's business strategy when it is a leader in its industry and uncommon fortitude to change the tried and true ways of doing business.[17] O'Reilly's decisive intervention and Shrontz's dogged efforts to uproot complacency can be applauded purely in terms of their likely positive impact on future corporate profitability. But these efforts also can benefit the ethical climate in each of these companies. The resulting improvements to operations and strategy reduce the likelihood of internal pressures for cutting ethical corners in order to achieve goals, as appears to have been the case for Sears. Moreover, a company's ability to provide good value to customers, job security to employees, and favorable returns to shareholders as the result of sound management practice has moral significance in itself.

Sears, as far as the author knows, had been a highly ethical firm over the years. But this company's recent experiences illustrate what can happen to moral climate when management has to fight for survival. While business decline does not necessarily cause moral decline, its likelihood increases as pressures and temptations for self-serving mount. As Beech-Nut so vividly portrayed, serious business difficulties can distort management's judgment and cause moral restraint to fall by the wayside.

Acting decisively, as O'Reilly did, is not without its own ethical risks. The challenge for the business leader is to bring about change without hurting people unfairly or pressuring them in ways that motivate improper actions. Management must take into account the wrenching experience that can accompany attempts to change business direction and must find ways to guard and reinforce ethical values in the process.

Major corporations regularly employ elaborate concepts and processes for strategic planning. Ironically, a formal process of strategic planning often does more to inhibit than to enhance innovative conceptual thinking. In all too many companies, strategic planning efforts produce little more than window dressing for poor thinking.[18] To be effective, strategic planning has to tap management's imagination, ingenuity, and daring. A corporate strategy is never optimal. There is always room for insight and invention. And for that to happen in a productive way, employees at all levels of an organization have to feel good about their work and the people they work with.

As in so many other regards, the chief executive sets the tone. People like Burke at J&J and Iverson at Nucor work hard to cultivate an atmosphere of trust. They show a care and concern for their subordinates that foster open communications. Their commitment to business success and their highly developed ability to encourage and support the operating unit managers without threatening the latters' freedom of action provide an organizational context motivating good management and timely strategic adaptations. Iverson's attitude toward risk-taking in Nucor Steel—typified by the

"Good managers [can] make bad decisions. They just ought to make more good decisions than bad" remark—speaks worlds about the crucial role of judgment in innovative business strategies.

When all is said and done, smart people who really like what they are doing, who like and respect their colleagues, who are prepared to take calculated risks, and who are members of a cohesive, well-run organization are what corporate excellence is all about. Business ethics is central to such an organization. Ethical standards, set by top management and fostered throughout the organization, can act to supercharge the engine of corporate performance.

Notes

Chapter 1

1. James Traub, "Into the Mouths of Babes," *New York Times Magazine,* July 24, 1988.

2. Ibid, pp. 38, 52.

3. Ibid, p. 20.

4. Chris Welles, "What Led Beech-Nut Down the Road to Disgrace?" *Business Week,* February 22, 1988, p. 125.

5. Ibid, p. 126.

6. "Into the Mouths of Babes," p. 53.

7. John R. Meyer and James M. Gustafson, editors, *The U.S. Business Corporation: An Institution in Transition* (New York: 1989).

8. Firms can be highly innovative in the short term while ignoring business ethics. One need only read Michael M. Lewis's account of Salomon Brothers in the 1980s for evidence of an impressive outpouring of innovation and risk taking in a macho, dog-eat-dog, highly fragmented organization [*Liar's Poker* (New York: 1989)]. The long-term viability of such an approach appears doubtful when compared to the uplifting forces that mutual respect and team spirit can engender over time.

Chapter 2

1. This point was clearly and forcefully made by the industrialist and public servant, Clarence B. Randall, *The Executive in Transition* (New York: 1967), p. 138.

. . . The difficulty is that the warning bell of their conscience does not ring as they make their decisions. They plunge into action without pausing to reflect upon the moral implications of the course to which they are committing themselves and their corporations. They have been carefully trained in engineering, cost accounting, pricing, human relations, and other phases of management, but not in ethics.

2. All names are disguised.

3. Disagreements on ethical matters as to what is at issue and how to deal with it—whether caused by different personal judgments or the nature of the situation—are commonplace in practice. One indication is given by an empirical study of the ethics of managing earnings that asked 200 managers in two firms and 108 internal auditors to indicate how ethical they judged 13 specific scenarios to be. It reported significant disagreement among the respondents for most of the scenarios, giving the following example.

> The general manager ordered his employees to defer all discretionary expenditures (e.g., travel, advertising, hiring, maintenance) from November and December until January so that his division could make its budgeted annual profit targets. Expected amount of deferral: $150,000

> Distribution of responses by the 308 managers and auditors:

Ethical practice	150
Questionable practice	52
Minor infraction	50
Serious infraction	42
Totally unethical	14

Kenneth A. Merchant and Joanne Rockness, "The Ethics of Managing Earnings: An Empirical Investigation," from a manuscript prepared for publication in the *Journal of Accounting and Public Policy*.

4. Touche Ross & Company, "Ethics in American Business," January 1988, p. 14.

5. The problem of conflicting views about the proper relationship between business and ethics is described by Kenneth E. Goodpaster, "The Moral Agenda of Corporate Leadership: Concepts and Research Techniques," in the D.S. MacNaughton Symposium Proceedings 1986, *The Ethical Dimensions of America's Corporate Practice: A Re-Examination* (New York: 1987), pp. 101–106.

6. Albert Z. Carr, "Is Business Bluffing Ethical?," *Harvard Business Review*, January-February 1968, p. 143. The author admonishes managers to make a sharp distinction between private ethical standards and the rules governing business practice.

7. Some people are guided primarily by moral principles, such as the Ten Commandments, which emphasize the actions (means) taken. With this *deontological* or *formalistic* perspective, it is wrong to lie or cheat, no matter what the circumstances. Other people believe that actions are not good or bad in themselves, but are to be judged by their consequences. The most influential theory within this *teleological* perspective is *utilitarianism*, which prescribes that we should act so as to create the greatest good for the greatest number of people. Other well-known ethical theories in-

clude *contractarianism*, based on the notion of a social contract, *relativism*, which regards all normative beliefs to be a function of a culture or the individual person. There is also the concept of *justice*, with a further delineation as to a proper basis of distribution—that is, giving to each person according to individual need, according to individual effort, in equal share, or according to some other measure. For a concise description of common ethical theories, see R. E. Reidenback and D. P. Robin, "Toward the Development of a Multidimensional Scale for Improving Evaluations of Business Ethics," *Journal of Business Ethics 9*, No. 78, August 1990, pp. 650–52.

8. Building a conceptual framework of moral development on foundations laid by Sigmund Freud, Jean Piaget, Erik Erikson, and others, the late Harvard psychologist Lawrence Kohlberg identifies six stages of moral reasoning to describe how persons define right from wrong:

1. Reward and punishment. (Parent to child: "You'll get spanked if you lie.")
2. Individualism and reciprocity. ("You scratch my back and I'll scratch yours.")
3. Interpersonal conformity. (We live up to what is expected of us by family and friends or by society in general.)
4. Law and order. (We meet our obligations in order to keep the system going as a whole.)
5. Social contract. ("The greatest good for the greatest number.")
6. Universal principles. (We have a sense of personal commitment to such universal moral principles as justice, equality, and the dignity of all human beings.)

Lawrence Kohlberg, *Essays on Moral Development, Vol. I: The Philosophy of Moral Development* (San Francisco: 1981).

This widely cited moral framework is based on the primacy and universality of reasoned principles. Carol Gilligan, in her insightful book on the psychology of women, proposes an alternative concept for moral understanding, based on situational considerations and a sense of empathy and responsibility to others [*In a Different Voice* (Cambridge, MA: 1982)]. One moral construct focuses more on how others deserve to be treated (rights), the other on how one should treat others (responsibilities). The difference might seem to be one of semantics (two sides of the same coin), but Gilligan argues persuasively that a person's mode of moral understanding is likely to have a profound impact on how he or she thinks about conflict and choice.

9. Barbara Ley Toffler, *Tough Choices* (New York: 1986), p. 20.

10. Frederick B. Bird and James A. Waters, "The Moral Muteness of Managers," *California Management Review*, Vol. 32, No. 1, Fall 1989, pp. 73–88.

11. James A. Waters and Frederick Bird, "The Moral Dimension of Organization Culture," *Journal of Business Ethics 6*, (1987), pp. 15–22.

This article develops a concept of moral stress, discussing its causes, consequences, and how it might be reduced.

12. Chris Argyris, *Overcoming Organizational Defenses* (Boston: 1990), p. 25.

13. Waters, "The Moral Dimension . . . ," p. 21.

14. See Jay W. Lorsch and E. MacIver, *Pawns or Potentates* (Boston: 1989) for a rich discussion of the workings of boards of directors for publicly owned U.S. corporations.

15. A study on how managers obtain information of strategic importance to the firm observed that much of what goes to senior people is unsolicited. People, both inside and outside the firm, would provide the information because they know of the executive's interests and have a convenient means to do so. [See Francis J. Aguilar, *Scanning the Business Environment* (New York: 1967), pp. 98–117.] This observation can provide an equally valuable lesson to managers attempting to inform themselves about ethical matters.

16. For a discerning discussion of this problem, see Chris Argyris, "Skilled Incompetence," *Harvard Business Review*, September-October 1986, pp. 74–79.

17. According to George C. Lodge, definitions of right and wrong are radically changing as American society experiences a major transition in ideology (the framework of ideas which a community uses to define values and to make them explicit). Referring to ideology as "a bridge which a community uses to get from timeless, universal noncontroversial notions such as survival, justice, economy, self-fulfillment and self-respect to the application of these motives in the real world," he explains how emerging concepts of rights and obligations add to the confusion about business ethics. "The Connection Between Ethics and Ideology," *Proceedings of the First National Conference on Business Ethics* (Waltham, MA: 1977), pp. 63–80.

Chapter 3

1. Arc welding machines, power sources, and consumable electrodes accounted for about 90 percent of the company's 1992 sales of $853 million. Lincoln also produces integral horsepower industrial electric motors. The various products are sold in both the domestic (56%) and international (44%) markets. The company's corporate headquarters and principal manufacturing facilities are located in the Cleveland, Ohio, area.

2. James F. Lincoln, "Our Philosophy," company publication, 1941.

3. James F. Lincoln, *Incentive Management* (Cleveland: 1951).

4. Lincoln Electric Company, 10K Report, 1992.

5. Norman Fast and Norman Berg, "The Lincoln Electric Company" (President and Fellows of Harvard College, 1975), p. 10.

6. Ibid., p. 10.

7. James F. Lincoln, "How Lincoln Motivated Men," *Civil Engineering—ASCE*, January 1973.

8. This section is largely excerpted from the Harvard Business school case "The Lincoln Electric Company," by Norman Fast and Norman Berg. The situation in early 1994 was essentially unchanged from that described in 1975.

9. William Irrgang, "The Lincoln Incentive Management Program," Lincoln Lecture Series, Arizona State University, 1972, p. 13.

10. *The Indianapolis Star*, December 5, 1982, p. 4C. The retirement benefits described for 1982 continue to apply in 1994.

11. High visibility executives began to park in an enclosed visitors parking area for security reasons following the kidnapping of Lincoln's former chairman in 1978.

12. Fast, *op. cit.*, p. 6.

13. John B. Matthews, Jr., "The Lincoln Electric Company (B)" (President and Fellows of Harvard College, 1978).

14. William Serrin, "The Way That Works at Lincoln," *The New York Times*, January 15, 1984.

15. The tests showed a low level of bio-availability. As a result, this promotional claim was toned down. Subsequently, the product was reformulated to increase the bio-availability of calcium.

16. All three staff units described as serving a safeguard function report to senior-level marketing executives. This reporting relationship ensures that they can operate with a degree of independence in dealing with the product divisions.

17. George C. S. Benson, "Codes of Ethics," *Journal of Business Ethics 8*, 1989, p. 305.

18. Dow Jones & Company, Inc., "Conflicts of Interest Policy," undated. This five-page policy statement was published over the name of Warren H. Phillips, then chairman of the board.

19. Donald H. Cressy and Charles A. Moore, "Managerial Values and Corporate Codes of Ethics," *California Management Review*, Vol. 25, No. 4, 1983, p. 54.

20. Benson, *op. cit*, pp. 308–309.

21. Laura L. Nash, "Johnson & Johnson's Credo" in *Corporate Ethics: A Prime Business Asset* (New York: 1988), pp. 95–96.

22. In 1982, seven people died after ingesting Tylenol capsules that had been laced with cyanide. Even though the poisoning had occurred outside J&J premises and was limited to the Chicago area, J&J withdrew all Tylenol capsules from the U.S. market at an estimated cost of $100 million. At the same time, the company initiated with the medical and pharmaceutical communities a comprehensive communication effort involving 2,500 employees throughout the J&J organization. This response

prompted the *Washington Post* to write that "Johnson & Johnson has succeeded in portraying itself to the public as a company willing to do what's right, regardless of cost."

23. "Johnson & Johnson's Credo," pp. 89–90.

24. All three companies justifiably pride themselves for conducting business in an ethical manner. The Credo and safeguards described for J&J and General Mills respectively represent only one element of a comprehensive structure fostering ethical behavior for each. For descriptions of the overall approach that J&J follows, see "Johnson & Johnson (A)" in Francis J. Aguilar, *General Managers in Action,* Second Edition (New York: 1992) pp 359–375, and Laura L. Nash, "Johnson & Johnson's Credo" in *Corporate Ethics: A Prime Business Asset* (New York: 1988), pp. 77–104. For General Mills, see Kenneth R. Andrews, "Ethics in Policy and Practice at General Mills," in *Corporate Ethics: A Prime Business Asset,* pp. 41–52. This company's commitment to community service is described in Chapter 4.

25. In a survey predominantly of directors and officers of large corporations, "increased concentration on short-term earnings" was rated as the second most important condition threatening to undermine American business ethics (just behind "decay in cultural and social institutions"). Touche Ross & Company, "Ethics in American Business," January 1988.

26. *Report of the National Commission on Fraudulent Financial Reporting,* 1987.

27. Kenneth A. Merchant, *Rewarding Results* (Boston: 1989).

Chapter 4

1. William A. Mehler, Jr., *Let the Buyer Have Faith: The Story of Armstrong* (Lancaster, PA: 1987), p. 5.

2. Ibid., p. 5.

3. Ibid., p. 79.

4. Richard O. von Werssowetz and Michael Beer, "Human Resources at Hewlett-Packard" (President and Fellows of Harvard College, Cambridge, MA.: 1982), Harvard Business School case 482–125.

5. Problems of this nature—when to do right in one regard results in doing wrong in another—are not uncommon. See Abbot Lawrence Lowell, *Conflicts of Principle* (Cambridge, MA: 1932).

6. "The New Dimensions of Corporate Citizenship," a talk by H. B. Atwater, Jr., given in Chicago on November 9, 1982, to the American Council of Life Insurance.

7. Kenneth R. Andrews, "Ethics in Policy and Practice at General Mills," *Corporate Ethics: A Prime Business Asset* (New York: 1988), p. 43.

8. "Charitable Investment: A New Mode of Corporate Citizenship," remarks by H.B. Atwater, Jr., given at the John F. Kennedy School of Government, Harvard University, November 16, 1987. In April 1991, General

Mills was one of only two corporations to receive a President's Volunteer Action Award, regarded as the nation's most prestigious award for community services.

9. Ibid.

10. For a more detailed account of the Altcare Program, see Timothy B. Blodgett, "Why General Mills Mixes in Health Care," *Harvard Business Review*, March-April 1989, pp. 32–34.

11. Andrews, pp. 45–46.

Chapter 5

1. *Forbes*, May 28, 1990, p. 200.

2. Pencil and paper tests that attempt to gauge honesty through multiple-choice questions are commonly used to supplement interviews for lower-ranking employees in security sensitive jobs, such as jewelry workers. Few companies that use psychological testing try to measure moral character by this means.

3. Founded in 1963, Mark Twain became a bank holding company offering a full range of financial services through its multiple banking offices in St. Louis and Kansas City, Missouri, and several units in neighboring states. It employed about 1,100 people in 1993.

4. Professional skills undoubtedly helped the Mark Twain recruiters in evaluating an applicant's rectitude. The three C's of lending were said to be "character, cash flow, and collateral," and Mark Twain deliberately emphasized a lender's character in making loans. The recruiters, in this instance, were skilled as bankers in judging character.

5. According to several professional experts in the field of industrial psychology and testing, an experienced interviewer can usually sense in the course of extensive interviews when people are frank in their responses and when they are holding back.

6. Frederick B. Bird and James A. Waters, "The Moral Muteness of Managers," *California Management Review*, Vol. 32, No. 1, Fall 1989, pp. 80 and 83. The statement ends with reference to managers. As argued in earlier chapters, participation in open discussion of business ethics should extend beyond management's ranks to include everyone affecting the firm's ethical behavior.

7. As in the other companies examined, ServiceMaster employed a comprehensive approach to motivating ethical business operations. This account focuses on its strategy for employee development, which was pivotal in transforming dispirited and disenfranchised service workers into involved and caring employees.

8. James L. Heskett, "ServiceMaster Industries, Inc." (President and Fellows of Harvard College, Cambridge, MA: 1987), Harvard Business School case 388-064.

9. Tim W. Ferguson, "Business World," *The Wall Street Journal*, May 8, 1990, p. A25.

10. *Forbes*, May 28, 1990, pp. 200, 202.

11. General Electric Company 1991 Annual Report. Welch had more than ethics in mind in his use of the word *values*. His concerns for quality, speed of action, risk taking, and the like were no doubt also at issue. Nonetheless, his analysis applies to the more limited point being made in this chapter.

12. *Cornerstone Five: Ethical Leadership* (Texas Instruments: 1992), p. 1.

Chapter 6

1. This observation was made by Robert W. Ackerman, *The Social Challenge to Business* (Cambridge, MA: 1975), p. 61, in connection with an in-depth study of how several companies dealt with major changes in societal expectations concerning such matters as equal employment opportunities and pollution abatement.

2. TI actually delayed joining DII until February 1988, when management was satisfied with the resolution of several issues, such as employee rights, the requirements for voluntary disclosure, and the identity of the independent organization to be responsible for public accountability.

3. "Sudden Change at General Dynamics," *Fortune*, June 24, 1985. The scandals, extending over a decade, were further dramatized by the machinations of Panegiotis Takis Veliotis, who allegedly had received many millions of dollars in kickbacks and bribes while serving as general manager of General Dynamics Electric Boat Division before fleeing the country. *Forbes*, January 16, 1984.

4. This account is largely drawn from an insightful case study published by Dr. Richard A. Barker, "An Evaluation of the Ethics Program at General Dynamics," *Journal of Business Ethics*, Volume 12, No. 3, March 1993, pp. 165–77. The Electronics Division, located in the San Diego area, employed about 3,500 people at the time of the study, representing approximately three percent of the company's employees. Dr. Barker had been a General Dynamics employee at middle management ranks for thirteen years in the time of the events recorded.

5. Ibid., p. 171.

6. Ibid., p. 172.

7. Ibid., p. 175.

8. Ibid.

9. General Dynamics, *Standards of Business Ethics and Conduct*, p. 1.

10. "Evaluation of the Ethics Program," p. 175.

11. The problem of senior line officers thwarting the efforts of staff

responsible for developing or administerig an ethics program can occur in any company, even those with a strong commitment to business ethics. The following account provides a vivid example of this with reference to insider trading of St. Regis shares just prior to a tender offer: "The compliance department at Goldman, which should have reviewed such trades by Freeman, proved as somnolent as Kidder, Peabody's or Drexel's. The low-prestige compliance officers at Goldman wouldn't dare challenge the trading of a powerful partner like Freeman. Goldman was hardly unique in that respect." James B. Stewart, *Den of Thieves* (New York: 1991), p. 160.

12. "Evalvation of the Ethics Program," p. 176.

13. In early 1993, Salomon Brothers was rumored to be considering rehiring John Meriwether to take charge of its troubled trading operations. This possibility prompted commentator Gary Weiss to conclude, "Hiring back their ace trader would signal the markets and regulators that Salomon still values profits over everything else—including public appearances." "Solly: Whatever Happened to Cleaning House?," *Business Week*, January 25, 1993, p. 43.

Chapter 7

1. "Taming the Monster: How Big Companies Can Change," *Wall Street Journal*, December 22, 1992, pp. A1 and A4.

2. Francis J. Aguilar and Arvind Bhambri, "Johnson & Johnson (A)" (President and Fellows of Harvard College, Cambridge, MA: 1983), contained in Francis J. Aguilar, *General Managers in Action*, Second Edition (New York: 1992), pp. 536–37.

3. *Wall Street Journal*, op. cit. An eleven-member executive committee is the principal senior management group in J&J responsible for the company's policies and operations.

4. Ibid.

5. Marvin Bower, former managing director of McKinsey & Company, described corporate culture as "the way we do things around here." *The Will to Manage* (New York: 1966). Embracing organizational values and philosophy as products of corporate culture, Schein argues that culture influences *everything* that the manager does, even his own thinking and feeling. Edgar H. Schein, *Organizational Culture and Leadership* (San Francisco: 1985), p. 314. For further discussion of the influence that organizational values have on individual members, see Amitai Etzioni, *The Moral Dimension: Toward a New Economics* (New York: 1988).

6. For a lively account of Nucor Steel's history and how it managed a high-risk, major innovation in steel making, see Richard Preston, *American Steel* (New York: 1991).

7. A perceptive cover story describing the experiences of an AIDS victim in Digital Equipment Corporation calls attention to the importance of putting into place early the needed support systems and the consider-

able effort and careful attention that must go into developing effective policies and practices for dealing with this emotional and touching issue. "Managing AIDS," *Business Week*, February 1, 1993, pp. 48–54.

8. These comments reflected the managerial *bête noire* of the 1980s. Increased shareholder activism and a corresponding responsiveness of publicly held corporate boards of directors has since gained prominence in this regard as powerful chief executive officers—such as Robert Stempel of General Motors, John Akers of IBM, Paul Lego of Westinghouse, and James Robinson of American Express—are ousted from their position.

9. *Wall Street Journal*, November 2, 1988.

10. *Fortune*, December 5, 1988.

11. *Business Week*, June 29, 1992, p. 38.

12. *Business Week*, August 3, 1992, p. 24.

13. For example, in mid-1993, Sears launched the biggest initial public stock offering ever by a U.S. company in selling approximately 20 percent of Allstate, which is the nation's second-largest car and home insurer, for roughly $2 billion. Earlier in the year, many Americans were saddened to learn that the once ubiquitous Sears catalog was to be discontinued after 97 years of operation.

14. *Business Week*, December 11, 1989, pp. 84–88.

15. "Running Ahead, But Running Scared," *Forbes*, May 13, 1991, pp. 38–40.

16. *Business Week*, March 1, 1993, p. 61.

17. For an account of one of the most comprehensive revitalization efforts in recent years, see the case studies "General Electric: Reg Jones and Jack Welch" and "General Electric—Preparing for the 1990s," in Francis J. Aguilar, *General Managers in Action* Second Edition, (New York: 1992), pp. 407–62. This remarkable transformation of one of the leading U.S. industrial firms began under Fred Borch in the late 1960s and is still underway more than 25 years later under Jack Welch.

18. A study of nine large companies led to the following assessment of formal planning as a tool for developing effective strategies:

> Although the formal planning approach is excellent for some purposes, it tends to focus unduly on measurable quantitative forces and to underemphasize the vital qualitative, organizational, and power/behavioral factors that so often determine strategic success in one situation versus another. It can easily become a rigid, cumbersome routine, used primarily as a basis for financial control, rather than a creative direction-setting challenge.

James Brian Quinn, *Strategies for Change: Logical Incrementalism* (Homewood, Ill: 1980), pp. 14–15.

Bibliography

Ackerman, Robert W., *The Social Challenge to Business* (Cambridge, MA: 1975).

Aguilar, Francis J., *General Managers in Action,* Second Edition (New York: 1992).

———— *Scanning the Business Environment* (New York: 1967).

———— "Bard MedSystems Division" (Cambridge, MA: 1987), Harvard Business School case 387-183.

———— "General Electric: Reg Jones and Jack Welch" (Cambridge, MA: 1991), Harvard Business School case 391-144.

———— "General Electric: Preparing for the 1990's" (Cambridge, MA: 1989), Harvard Business School case 390-091.

———— and Arvin Bhambri, *Johnson & Johnson (A)* (Cambridge, MA: 1983), Harvard Business School case 384-053.

Andrews, Kenneth R., "Ethics in Policy and Practice at General Mills," in *Corporate Ethics: A Prime Business Asset* (New York: 1988), pp. 41–52.

Argyris, Chris, *Overcoming Organizational Defenses* (Boston: 1990).

———— "Skilled Incompetence," *Harvard Business Review,* September-October 1986, pp. 74–79.

Barker, Richard A., "An Evaluation of the Ethics Program at General Dynamics," *Journal of Business Ethics,* Vol. 12, No. 3, March 1993, pp. 165–77.

Benson, George C. S., "Codes of Ethics," *Journal of Business Ethics,* Vol. 8, No. 5, May 1989, pp. 305–19.

Bird, Frederick B. and James A. Waters, "The Moral Muteness of Managers," *California Management Review,* Volume 32, No. 1, Fall 1989, pp. 73–88.

Blodgett, Timothy B., "Why General Mills Mixes in Health Care," *Harvard Business Review,* March-April 1989, pp. 32–34.

Bower, Marvin, *The Will to Manage* (New York: 1966).

Carr, Albert Z., "Is Business Bluffing Ethical?," *Harvard Business Review*, January–February, 1968, pp. 143–153.

Cressy, Donald H. and Charles A. Moore, "Managerial Values and Corporate Codes of Ethics," *California Management Review*, Vol. 25, No. 4, 1983, pp. 53–77.

Etzioni, Amitai, *The Moral Dimension: Toward a New Economics* (New York: 1988).

Fast, Norman and Norman Berg, "The Lincoln Electric Company" (Cambridge, MA: 1975), Harvard Business School case 376-028.

Gilligan, Carol, *In a Different Voice* (Cambridge, MA: 1982).

Goodpaster, Kenneth E., "The Moral Agenda of Corporate Leadership: Concepts and Research Techniques," in the D. S. MacNaughton Symposium Proceedings, 1986, *The Ethical Dimensions of America's Corporate Practice: A Re-Examination* (Syracuse University: 1987) pp. 101–106.

Heskett, James L., "Service Master Industries, Inc." (Cambridge, MA: 1987), Harvard Business School case 388-064.

Kohlberg, Lawrence, *Essays on Moral Development, Volume 1: The Philosophy of Moral Development,* (San Francisco: 1981).

Lewis, Michael M., *Liar's Poker* (New York: 1989).

Lincoln, James F., *Incentive Management* (Cleveland: 1951).

Lodge, George C., "The Connection Between Ethics and Ideology," *Proceedings of the First National Conference on Business Ethics* (Waltham, MA: 1977), pp. 63–80.

Lorsch, Jay W. and E. MacIver, *Pawns or Potentates* (Boston, MA: 1989).

Lowell, Abbot Lawrence, *Conflicts of Principle* (Cambridge, MA: 1932).

Matthews, John B., Jr., "The Lincoln Electric Company (B)" (Cambridge, MA: 1978), Harvard Business School case 378-216.

Mehler, William A., Jr., *Let the Buyer Have Faith: The Story of Armstrong* (Lancaster, PA: 1987).

Merchant, Kenneth A., *Rewarding Results* (Boston, MA: 1989).

Meyer, John R. and James M. Gustafson, editors, *The U.S. Business Corporation: An Institution in Transition* (New York: 1989).

Nash, Laura L., "Johnson & Johnson's Credo" in *Corporate Ethics: A Prime Business Asset* (New York: 1988).

Preston, Richard, *American Steel* (New York: 1991).

Quinn, James Brian, *Strategies for Change: Logical Incrementalism* (Homewood, IL: 1980).

Randell, Clarence B., *The Executive in Transition* (New York, 1967).

Reidenbeck, R.E., and D.P. Robin, "Toward the Development of a Multidimensional Scale for Improving Evaluations of Business Ethics," *Journal of Business Ethics,* Vol. 9, No. 8, August 1990, pp. 639–53.

Schein, Edgar H., *Organizational Culture and Leadership* (San Francisco: 1985).

Stewart, James B., *Den of Thieves* (New York: 1991).

Toffler, Barbara Ley, *Tough Choices* (New York: 1986).

Touche Ross & Company, "Ethics in American Business," January 1988.

von Werssowetz, Richard O. and Michael Beer, "Human Resources at Hewlett-Packard" (Cambridge, MA: 1982), Harvard Business School case 482–125.

Waters, James A. and Frederick Bird, "The Moral Dimension of Organizational Culture," *Journal of Business Ethics*, Vol. 6, No. 1, pp. 15–22.

Index